To the Peoples of the World
A Bahá'í Statement on Peace

To the Peoples of the World

A Bahá'í Statement on

Peace

by the
Universal House of Justice

Published by:
THE ASSOCIATION FOR BAHÁ'Í STUDIES
34 Copernicus Street
Ottawa, Ontario, Canada
K1N 7K4

ISBN 0-920904-15-7

©1986
Printed in Canada

*"World peace is not only possible but inevitable.
It is the next stage in the evolution of this planet . . . ."*

The Universal House of Justice

CONTENTS

Introduction ix
Foreword xiii
Part One: To the Peoples of the World 1
Part Two: Annotations
   The Quest for Peace 29
   Technology: For War or Peace? 34
   The Spectre of War 37
   Aggression and Human Nature 39
   Collective Growth of Mankind 43
   The Transcendent Nature of the Human Spirit ... 45
   Progressive Revelation 47
   Role of Religion in Establishing World Peace 50
   The Golden Rule 53
   Substitute Faiths 55
   Disarmament 57
   Declarations and Conventions of the United Nations 59
   Barriers to Peace:
      Racism 62
      Disparity between Rich and Poor 63
      Unbridled Nationalism 65
      Religious Strife 67
   Important Prerequisites for Peace:
      Equality of the Sexes 68
      Universal Education 69
      Improved Global Communication 71
   Unity: The Cardinal Prerequisite for Peace 72
   Towards a New World Order 74
   Consultation and Conflict Resolution 77
   The Experience of the Bahá'í Community 80
Appreciations 85
About the Contributors 89
Select Bahá'í Bibliography 91

INTRODUCTION

BACKGROUND

On October 24, 1985, the Universal House of Justice, the supreme governing body of the Bahá'í Faith, addressed a statement to the peoples of the world on the theme of peace. This historic undertaking represents the most far-reaching effort in the area of peace that has been advanced by the Bahá'í community since its inception in the mid-nineteenth century.

One of the fundamental objectives of the Bahá'í Faith is the establishment of world peace within the framework of a unified, spiritually enlightened new world order. During his own life, Bahá'u'lláh (1817–1892), the prophet-founder of the Bahá'í Faith, addressed a number of letters to the kings, religious leaders and peoples of the world, outlining the main prerequisites for world peace. His voluminous writings stressed, even at that early date, the imperative need for a world order based on justice, the eradication of all forms of prejudice, the equality of the sexes, and recognition of the essential harmony between science and religion. Other principles enunciated by Bahá'u'lláh included the creation of universal institutions designed to foster the unity of mankind, and the search for a solution to world economic problems through consideration of the spiritual dimensions of human life.

'Abdu'l-Bahá (1844–1921), the eldest son and immediate appointed successor to Bahá'u'lláh, likewise dedicated his life to these objectives. In a series of remarkable lectures in Europe and North America during the years 1911–1913, and in thousands of letters to Bahá'ís around the world throughout his lifetime, he further elaborated upon Bahá'í teachings in regard to the establishment of peace. These efforts were enhanced and given more specific focus by Shoghi Effendi (1897–1957), the successor to 'Abdu'l-Bahá, who guided the Bahá'í community during perhaps the most turbulent decades in the history of mankind and took up the task of developing a united, peaceful Bahá'í world community, enriched and beautified by the diversity of its peoples and cultures.

Now the Universal House of Justice has reissued this call to mankind, and Bahá'í communities around the world have responded with vigour and enthusiasm. Since October 24, 1985, the fortieth anniversary of the establishment of the United Nations, Bahá'ís have presented the statement on peace to the Secretary-General of the United Nations as well as to a large number of states and governments throughout the world. Presentations will continue until all governments and many leaders of humanity in various fields have received the message. It is hoped, too, that in this process a large number of peoples of the world will have become acquainted with the contents of this statement.

OVERVIEW

This weighty and comprehensive document identifies several themes and concepts cardinal to the Bahá'í understanding of human nature and the process of the unfoldment of human civilization. Among these are the concepts of the collective growth of mankind, the spiritual and noble nature of man, the necessity for the unity of mankind as the prerequisite for peace, and the progressive nature of divine revelation.

Recognizing that the establishment of peace has been the quest of many people throughout history, the Universal House of Justice asserts that its achievement has become possible only now, with humanity's coming of age. Impelled by the forces of growth inherent in all creation, including mankind as a whole, humanity is now traversing its age of adolescence and approaching an era in which world peace will become not only possible but inevitable. However, as humanity nears its age of maturity, approaches to its problems must be modified. One of the most urgent of these problems is the current climate of discord, antagonism and readiness for war existing in the world—a negative factor tempered by the increasing awareness of the grave perils inherent in this current attitude. The choice which faces us now is whether to foster the establishment of world peace through a process characterized by cooperation, collaboration and consultation, or, alternatively, to allow the destructive forces of competition, enmity and mistrust to lead mankind on a path to such destruction that the nations and peoples of the world will, out of desperation, accept peace as their last resort.

The assertion by the Universal House of Justice that peace is inevitable is based on the recognition that with the advent of maturity comes much greater desire and ability for cooperation, harmony, and mutuality. The movement towards unity identified in the statement has a history as old as mankind itself, beginning with the development of the family and the tribe, and progressing through the establishment of the city-state and the nation until the culmination of the process today, with the era of uniting nations into one world commonwealth in the framework of a new world order. World unity, therefore, is the prime prerequisite for peace, and without it the quest for peace, however powerful and sincere, will remain a quest and nothing more.

The advent of the maturity of mankind not only lays the foundations for the establishment of unity and therefore world peace, but also hastens the spiritualization of life. This is a circular process, as greater maturity facilitates more spirituality, and a spiritual lifestyle brings about a greater degree of maturity. This circular relationship will ultimately provide us with an opportunity to demonstrate, for the first time on a collective basis, the human qualities of nobility and spirituality. Thus, the coming of age of mankind is not only the harbinger of the era of unity but also of our freedom from the bondage of instinctual and animalistic forces most powerful during our childhood and adolescence. With this freedom we, at last, shall move from the predominantly materialistic phase of our life and begin the era of our spiritual enlightenment. Thus, the current misconceptions about human nature, perceiving it to be aggressive and violent, are due to the disregard shown for the process of the collective growth of mankind. The aggression, self-centredness, competition and war characterizing the annals of human history are reflections of the behaviour of humanity during its stages of childhood and adolescence. A mature and healthy society will, no doubt, replace aggression with love, self-centredness with service to others, competition with cooperation, and war with peace. The Universal House of Justice's call is for the affirmation of the noble and spiritual nature of humanity, which is totally interdependent with the cause of unity and peace.

In the statement, two invitations are extended to the leaders and peoples of the world. The specific invitation to the leaders is for the convocation of a world assembly, attended by heads of governments and rulers of humanity. The second invitation, to the peoples of the world, offers for study the experience of the world-wide Bahá'í community as one prototype for the creation of a united and peaceful world. The Bahá'í experience is interesting, not only because of the kind of communities which have evolved, but also for the manner in which they deal with violence. The case of the Bahá'ís of Iran and their response to tyranny and oppression is one excellent contemporary example of the application of the Bahá'í teachings on the nobility of human nature and the ultimate victory of the forces of love and unity over those of hatred and separation.

FORMAT

The book is composed of three parts: the statement by the Universal House of Justice, a glossary of themes, and a number of comments by world-renowned thinkers on the subject of peace, including a foreword by Dr. Ervin Laszlo of the Club of Rome and appreciations by Professor Johan Galtung of Princeton University, and Dr. Rodrigo Carazo of the United Nations University for Peace. In order to facilitate study, all references and quotations found in the text of the peace statement itself have been annotated directly following the text. In addition, some of the major themes and concepts are identified in the margins and are elaborated upon in the glossary section, with quotations from various sources on the same theme. The intention here is not to provide an exhaustive list of sources, but rather to assist and encourage readers to conduct their own research and to provide them with references to the topics identified.

The comments on the statement, by some of the distinguished statesmen and scholars of our time, reflect not only their views about the importance of world peace and the prerequisites for its arrival, but also the urgency of its achievement. The insights, enlightenment and courage of leaders in all spheres will assist humanity to traverse this, its age of adolescence, with as little destruction and as much creativity as possible. For their contributions to this process we are most grateful.

HOSSAIN DANESH
Editor

FOREWORD

The Bahá'í call for peace comes at a crucial moment in the history of humanity. Peace in the contemporary world is no longer an option but a necessity. All leaders and peoples of the world must come to realize this fact, and achieve the maturity which the Bahá'í Faith foresees for the coming of age of humanity.

To achieve peace we need a new orientation of thought and a new knowledge of the dynamics of change in the history of human society. Both have been grasped in their essence in the Bahá'í teachings. Conventional wisdom sees conflict as the warp and woof of history, punctuated by wars and relieved by temporary respites when swords are shielded and guns are silent. In conventional terms peace is merely truce; war, with ultimate conquest or subjugation, victory or defeat, is the paradigm. Contemporary governments seek security through force of arms: they aspire to peace but prepare for war.

But this concept of history, this view of the human condition, is not only false; it is a menace to life and civilization. In a world where the technologies of destruction can destroy the human population of the globe twenty times over, and where the technologies of production, services and communication are sophisticated but vulnerable, force is not an instrument of security but of genocide. In our times we can only survive, and our civilization can only flower, if we reorient the conventional wisdom and achieve the new insights which have been proclaimed by the Bahá'í Faith and which are now also supported by the latest discoveries of the empirical sciences.

Bahá'ís proclaim that the most important condition that can bring about peace is unity—the unity of families, of nations, and of the great currents of thought and inquiry that we denote science and religion. Maturity, in turn, is a prerequisite for such unity. This is evolutionary thinking, and its validity is shown by the new theories which emerge from nonequilibrium thermodynamics, dynamical systems theory, cybernetics, and the related sciences of complexity. They are supported by detailed empirical investigations in such fields as physical cosmology, paleobiological macroevolutionary theory, and new trends in historiography.

The new scientific findings underscore the Bahá'í proclamations in regard both the overall direction of historical development—which is from primitive bands of nomadic hunters-gatherers to modern post-industrial societies and the global web of interdependence weaved by them which must, if given the chance, lead ultimately to global unity, and the overall mode of historical development, which is always beset with crises and discontinuities but is also endowed with the freedom of selecting alternative outcomes. In society as in nature, change is sudden and discontinuous, and offers multiple trajectories. Conscious human beings can explore and make use of the alternatives and choose the one that leads evolution's preferred direction with the least possible suffering and violence.

If a group of people in possession of the ideas and the faith of the Bahá'í act in concert and with conscious knowledge of the dynamics of the historical juncture in which humanity now finds itself, they can decisively influence and change the present course of history. In the language of the new sciences of evolution, they can be the small, initially peripheral fluctuation which can be suddenly amplified in a complex dynamical system when that system becomes critically unstable, and which, amplified and spreading, can determine the course of the coming bifurcation. Acting with sound knowledge, solid faith and firm determination, men and women of good will can load the dice of social change, bias the statistics of evolutionary transformation, and achieve a humanistic end that is consistent with the great patterns and modalities of evolution that hold good on Earth as in the vast reaches of the cosmos. Maturity does not come without the turbulence of adolescence; dynamic stability on a new plane of organization cannot be achieved without critical instability and bifurcation on lesser organizational levels.

People of good will everywhere need to heed the call for world peace by the Bahá'í community and reflect on its deeper significance in light of their own perceptions, traditions, and the emerging theories of the empirical sciences. Then, through the multiplicity of approaches a common insight will crystallize, a shared way will be found. Humanity can set out on the road to a greater wisdom, a fuller maturity, if only it is given the opportunity to search its cultures and wisdoms, and reflect on its time and place in the biospheric, indeed in the cosmic, order of physical, biological and sociocultural reality.

ERVIN LASZLO
October 1985

Part One
To The Peoples of the World

Statement of the Universal House of Justice
October 1985

To The Peoples of the World

The Great Peace towards which people of good will throughout the centuries have inclined their hearts, of which seers and poets for countless generations have expressed their vision, and for which from age to age the sacred scriptures of mankind have constantly held the promise, is now at long last within the reach of the nations. For the first time in history it is possible for everyone to view the entire planet, with all its myriad diversified peoples, in one perspective. World peace is not only possible but inevitable. It is the next stage in the evolution of this planet—in the words of one great thinker, "the planetization of mankind."[1]

The Quest For Peace

Whether peace is to be reached only after unimaginable horrors precipitated by humanity's stubborn clinging to old patterns of behaviour, or is to be embraced now by an act of consultative will, is the choice before all who inhabit the earth. At this critical juncture when the intractable problems confronting nations have been fused into one common concern for the whole world, failure to stem the tide of conflict and disorder would be unconscionably irresponsible.

Among the favourable signs are the steadily growing strength of the steps towards world order taken initially near the beginning of this century in the creation of the League of Nations, succeeded by the more broadly based United Nations Organization; the achievement since the Second World War of independence by the majority of all the nations on earth, indicating the completion of the process of nation building, and the involvement of these fledgling nations with older ones in matters of mutual concern; the consequent vast increase in co-operation among hitherto isolated and antagonistic peoples and groups in international undertakings in the scientific, educational, legal, economic and cultural fields; the rise in recent decades of an unprecedented number of international humanitarian organizations; the spread of women's and youth movements calling for an end to war; and the spontaneous spawning of widening networks of ordinary people seeking understanding through personal communication.

The scientific and technological advances occurring in this unusually blessed century portend a great surge forward in the social evolution of the planet, and indicate the means by which the practical problems of humanity may be solved. They provide, indeed, the very means for the administration of the complex life of a united world. Yet barriers persist. Doubts, misconceptions, prejudices, suspicions and narrow self-interest beset nations and peoples in their relations one to another.

Technology: For War or Peace?

It is out of a deep sense of spiritual and moral duty that we are impelled at this opportune moment to invite your attention to the penetrating insights first communicated to the rulers of mankind more than a century ago by Bahá'u'lláh, Founder of the Bahá'í Faith, of which we are the Trustees.

"The winds of despair," Bahá'u'lláh wrote, "are, alas, blowing from every direction, and the strife that divides and afflicts the human race is daily increasing. The signs of impending convulsions and chaos can now be discerned, inasmuch as the prevailing order appears to be lamentably defective."[2] This prophetic judgement has been amply confirmed by the common experience of humanity. Flaws in the prevailing order are conspicuous in the inability of sovereign states organized as United Nations to exorcize the spectre of war, the threatened collapse of the international economic order, the spread of anarchy and terrorism, and the intense suffering which these and other afflictions are causing to increasing millions. Indeed, so much have aggression and conflict come to characterize our social, economic and religious systems, that many have succumbed to the view that such behaviour is intrinsic to human nature and therefore ineradicable.

The Spectre of War

Aggression and Human Nature

With the entrenchment of this view, a paralyzing contradiction has developed in human affairs. On the one hand, people of all nations proclaim not only their readiness but their longing for peace and harmony, for an end to the harrowing apprehensions tormenting their daily lives. On the other, uncritical assent is given to the proposition that human beings are incorrigibly selfish and aggressive and thus incapable of erecting a social system at once progressive and peaceful, dynamic and harmonious, a system giving free play to individual creativity and initiative but based on co-operation and reciprocity.

As the need for peace becomes more urgent, this fundamental contradiction, which hinders its realization, demands a reassessment of the assumptions upon which the commonly-held view of mankind's historical predicament is based. Dispassionately examined, the evidence reveals that such conduct, far from expressing man's true self, represents a distortion of the human spirit. Satisfaction on this point will enable all people to set in motion constructive social forces which, because they are consistent with human nature, will encourage harmony and co-operation instead of war and conflict.

To choose such a course is not to deny humanity's past but to understand it. The Bahá'í Faith regards the current world confusion and calamitous condition in human affairs as a natural phase in an organic process leading ultimately and irresistibly to the unification of the human race in a single social order whose boundaries are those of the planet. The human race, as a distinct, organic unit, has passed through evolutionary stages analogous to the stages of infancy and childhood in the lives of its individual members, and is now in the culminating period of its turbulent adolescence approaching its long-awaited coming of age.

Collective Growth of Mankind

A candid acknowledgement that prejudice, war and exploitation have been the expression of immature stages in a vast historical process and that the human race is today experiencing the unavoidable tumult which marks its collective coming of age is not a reason for despair but a prerequisite to undertaking the stupendous enterprise of building a peaceful world. That such an enterprise is possible, that the necessary constructive forces do exist, that unifying social structures can be erected, is the theme we urge you to examine.

Whatever suffering and turmoil the years immediately ahead may hold, however dark the immediate circumstances, the Bahá'í community believes that humanity can confront this supreme trial with confidence in its ultimate outcome. Far from signaling the end of civilization, the convulsive changes towards which humanity is being ever more rapidly impelled will serve to release the "potentialities inherent in the station of man" and reveal "the full measure of his destiny on earth, the innate excellence of his reality."[3]

I

The endowments which distinguish the human race from all other forms of life are summed up in what is known as the human spirit; the mind is its essential quality. These endowments have enabled humanity to build civilizations and to prosper materially. But such accomplishments alone have never satisfied the human spirit, whose mysterious nature inclines it towards transcendence, a reaching towards an invisible realm, towards the ultimate reality, that unknowable essence of essences called God. The religions brought to mankind by a succession of spiritual luminaries have been the primary link between humanity and that ultimate reality, and have galvanized and refined mankind's capacity to achieve spiritual success together with social progress.

The Transcendent Nature of the Human Spirit

Progressive Revelation

No serious attempt to set human affairs aright, to achieve world peace, can ignore religion. Man's perception and practice of it are largely the stuff of history. An eminent historian described religion as a "faculty of human nature."[4] That the perversion of this faculty has contributed to much of the confusion in society and the conflicts in and between individuals can hardly be denied. But neither can any fair-minded observer discount the preponderating influence exerted by religion on the vital expressions of civilization. Furthermore, its indispensability to social order has repeatedly been demonstrated by its direct effect on laws and morality. Writing of religion as a social force, Bahá'u'lláh said: "Religion is the greatest of all means for the establishment of order in the world and for the peaceful contentment of all that dwell therein."[5] Referring to the eclipse or corruption of religion, he wrote: "Should the lamp of religion be obscured, chaos and confusion will ensue, and the lights of fairness, of justice, of tranquillity and peace cease to shine."[6] In an enumeration of such consequences the Bahá'í writings point out that the "perversion of human nature, the degradation of human conduct, the corruption and dissolution of human institutions, reveal themselves, under such circumstances, in their worst and most revolting aspects. Human character is debased, confidence is shaken, the nerves of discipline are relaxed, the voice of human conscience is stilled, the sense of decency and shame is obscured, conceptions of duty, of solidarity, of reciprocity and loyalty are distorted, and the very feeling of peacefulness, of joy and of hope is gradually extinguished."[7]

Role of Religion in Achieving World Peace

If, therefore, humanity has come to a point of paralyzing conflict it must look to itself, to its own negligence, to the siren voices to which it has listened, for the source of the misunderstandings and confusion perpetrated in the name of religion. Those who have held blindly and selfishly to their particular orthodoxies, who have imposed on their votaries erroneous and conflicting interpretations of the pronouncements of the Prophets of God, bear heavy responsibility for this confusion—a confusion compounded by the artificial barriers erected between faith and reason, science and religion. For from a fair-minded examination of the actual utterances of the Founders of the great religions, and of the social milieus in which they were obliged to carry out their missions, there is nothing to support the contentions and prejudices deranging the religious communities of mankind and therefore all human affairs.

The teaching that we should treat others as we

ourselves would wish to be treated, an ethic variously repeated in all the great religions, lends force to this latter observation in two particular respects: it sums up the moral attitude, the peace-inducing aspect, extending through these religions irrespective of their place or time of origin; it also signifies an aspect of unity which is their essential virtue, a virtue mankind in its disjointed view of history has failed to appreciate. *The Golden Rule*

Had humanity seen the Educators of its collective childhood in their true character, as agents of one civilizing process, it would no doubt have reaped incalculably greater benefits from the cumulative effects of their successive missions. This, alas, it failed to do.

The resurgence of fanatical religious fervour occurring in many lands cannot be regarded as more than a dying convulsion. The very nature of the violent and disruptive phenomena associated with it testifies to the spiritual bankruptcy it represents. Indeed, one of the strangest and saddest features of the current outbreak of religious fanaticism is the extent to which, in each case, it is undermining not only the spiritual values which are conducive to the unity of mankind but also those unique moral victories won by the particular religion it purports to serve.

However vital a force religion has been in the history of mankind, and however dramatic the current resurgence of militant religious fanaticism, religion and religious institutions have, for many decades, been viewed by increasing numbers of people as irrelevant to the major concerns of the modern world. In its place they have turned either to the hedonistic pursuit of material satisfactions or to the following of man-made ideologies designed to rescue society from the evident evils under which it groans. All too many of these ideologies, alas, instead of embracing the concept of the oneness of mankind and promoting the increase of concord among different peoples, have tended to deify the state, to subordinate the rest of mankind to one nation, race or class, to attempt to suppress all discussion and interchange of ideas, or to callously abandon starving millions to the operations of a market system that all too clearly is aggravating the plight of the majority of mankind, while enabling small sections to live in a condition of affluence scarcely dreamed of by our forebears. How tragic is the record of the substitute faiths that the worldly-wise of our age have created. In the massive disillusionment of entire populations who have been taught to worship at their altars can be read history's irreversible verdict on their value. The fruits these doctrines have produced, after decades of an increasingly unrestrained exercise of power by those who owe their ascendancy in human affairs to them, are the social and economic ills that blight every region of our world in the closing years of the twentieth century. Underlying all these outward afflictions is the spiritual damage reflected in the apathy that has gripped the mass of the peoples of all nations and by the extinction of hope in the hearts of deprived and anguished millions.

Substitute Faiths

The time has come when those who preach the dogmas of materialism, whether of the east or the west, whether of capitalism or socialism, must give account of the moral stewardship they have presumed to exercise. Where is the "new world" promised by these ideologies? Where is the international peace to whose ideals they proclaim their devotion? Where are the breakthroughs into new realms of cultural achievement produced by the aggrandizement of this race, of that nation or of a particular class? Why is the vast majority of the world's peoples sinking ever deeper into hunger and wretchedness when wealth on a scale undreamed of by the Pharaohs, the Caesars, or even the imperialist powers of the nineteenth century is at the disposal of the present arbiters of human affairs?

Most particularly, it is in the glorification of material pursuits, at once the progenitor and common feature of all such ideologies, that we find the roots which nourish the falsehood that human beings are incorrigibly selfish and aggressive. It is here that the ground must be cleared for the building of a new world fit for our descendants.

That materialistic ideals have, in the light of experience, failed to satisfy the needs of mankind calls for an honest acknowledgement that a fresh effort must now be made to find the solutions to the agonizing problems of the planet. The intolerable conditions pervading society bespeak a common failure of all, a circumstance which tends to incite rather than relieve the entrenchment on every side. Clearly, a common remedial effort is urgently required. It is primarily a matter of attitude. Will humanity continue in its waywardness, holding to outworn concepts and unworkable assumptions? Or will its leaders, regardless of ideology, step forth and, with a resolute will, consult together in a united search for appropriate solutions?

Those who care for the future of the human race may well ponder this advice: "If long-cherished ideals and time-honoured institutions, if certain social assumptions and religious formulae have ceased to promote the welfare of the generality of mankind, if they no longer minister to the needs of a continually evolving humanity, let them be swept away and relegated to the limbo of obsolescent and forgotten doctrines. Why should these, in a world subject to the immutable law of change and decay, be exempt from the deterioration that must needs overtake every human institution? For legal standards, political and economic theories are solely designed to safeguard the interests of humanity as a whole, and not humanity to be crucified for the preservation of the integrity of any particular law or doctrine."[8]

Statement of the
Universal House of Justice

II

Banning nuclear weapons, prohibiting the use of poison gases, or outlawing germ warfare will not remove the root causes of war. However important such practical measures obviously are as elements of the peace process, they are in themselves too superficial to exert enduring influence. Peoples are ingenious enough to invent yet other forms of warfare, and to use food, raw materials, finance, industrial power, ideology, and terrorism to subvert one another in an endless quest for supremacy and dominion. Nor can the present massive dislocation in the affairs of humanity be resolved through the settlement of specific conflicts or disagreements among nations. A genuine universal framework must be adopted.

Disarmament

Certainly, there is no lack of recognition by national leaders of the world-wide character of the problem, which is self-evident in the mounting issues that confront them daily. And there are the accumulating studies and solutions proposed by many concerned and enlightened groups as well as by agencies of the United Nations, to remove any possibility of ignorance as to the challenging requirements to be met. There is, however, a paralysis of will; and it is this that must be carefully examined and resolutely dealt with. This paralysis is rooted, as we have stated, in a deep-seated conviction of the inevitable quarrelsomeness of mankind, which has led to the reluctance to entertain the possibility of subordinating national self-interest to the requirements of world order, and in an unwillingness to face courageously the far-reaching implications of establishing a united world authority. It is also traceable to the incapacity of largely ignorant and subjugated masses to articulate their desire for a new order in which they can live in peace, harmony and prosperity with all humanity.

The tentative steps towards world order, especially since World War II, give hopeful signs. The increasing tendency of groups of nations to formalize relationships which enable them to co-operate in matters of mutual interest suggests that eventually all nations could overcome this paralysis. The Association of South East Asian Nations, the Caribbean Community and Common Market, the Central American Common Market, the Council for Mutual Economic Assistance, the European Communities, the League of Arab States, the Organization of African Unity, the Organization of American States, the South Pacific Forum—all the joint endeavours represented by such organizations prepare the path to world order.

The increasing attention being focused on some of the most deep-rooted problems of the planet is yet another hopeful sign. Despite the obvious shortcomings of the United Nations, the more than two score declarations and conventions adopted by that organization, even where governments have not been enthusiastic in their commitment, have given ordinary people a sense of a new lease on life. *Declarations and Conventions of the United Nations* The Universal Declaration of Human Rights, the Convention on the Prevention and Punishment of the Crime of Genocide, and the similar measures concerned with eliminating all forms of discrimination based on race, sex or religious belief; upholding the rights of the child; protecting all persons against being subjected to torture; eradicating hunger and malnutrition; using scientific and technological progress in the interest of peace and the benefit of mankind—all such measures, if courageously enforced and expanded, will advance the day when the spectre

Statement of the
Universal House of Justice

of war will have lost its power to dominate international relations. There is no need to stress the significance of the issues addressed by these declarations and conventions. However, a few such issues, because of their immediate relevance to establishing world peace, deserve additional comment.

Racism, one of the most baneful and persistent evils, is a major barrier to peace. Its practice perpetrates too outrageous a violation of the dignity of human beings to be countenanced under any pretext. Racism retards the unfoldment of the boundless potentialities of its victims, corrupts its perpetrators, and blights human progress. Recognition of the oneness of mankind, implemented by appropriate legal measures, must be universally upheld if this problem is to be overcome.

Barriers to Peace

Racism

The inordinate disparity between rich and poor, a source of acute suffering, keeps the world in a state of instability, virtually on the brink of war. Few societies have dealt effectively with this situation. The solution calls for the combined application of spiritual, moral and practical approaches. A fresh look at the problem is required, entailing consultation with experts from a wide spectrum of disciplines, devoid of economic and ideological polemics, and involving the people directly affected in the decisions that must urgently be made. It is an issue that is bound up not only with the necessity for eliminating extremes of wealth and poverty but also with those spiritual verities the understanding of which can produce a new universal attitude. Fostering such an attitude is itself a major part of the solution.

Disparity between Rich and Poor

Unbridled nationalism, as distinguished from a sane and legitimate patriotism, must give way to a wider loyalty, to the love of humanity as a whole. Bahá'u'lláh's statement is: "The earth is but one country, and mankind its citizens."⁹ The concept of world citizenship is a direct result of the contraction of the world into a single neighbourhood

Unbridled Nationalism

12

Statement of the
Universal House of Justice

through scientific advances and of the indisputable interdependence of nations. Love of all the world's peoples does not exclude love of one's country. The advantage of the part in a world society is best served by promoting the advantage of the whole. Current international activities in various fields which nurture mutual affection and a sense of solidarity among peoples need greatly to be increased.

Religious strife, throughout history, has been the cause of innumerable wars and conflicts, a major blight to progress, and is increasingly abhorrent to the people of all faiths and no faith. *Religious Strife* Followers of all religions must be willing to face the basic questions which this strife raises, and to arrive at clear answers. How are the differences between them to be resolved, both in theory and in practice? The challenge facing the religious leaders of mankind is to contemplate, with hearts filled with the spirit of compassion and a desire for truth, the plight of humanity, and to ask themselves whether they cannot, in humility before their Almighty Creator, submerge their theological differences in a great spirit of mutual forbearance that will enable them to work together for the advancement of human understanding and peace.

The emancipation of women, the achievement of full equality between the sexes, is one of the most important, though less acknowledged prerequisites of peace. The denial of such equality perpetrates an injustice against one half of the world's population and promotes in men harmful attitudes and habits that are carried from the family to the workplace, to *Important Prerequisites for Peace* *Equality of the Sexes* political life, and ultimately to international relations. There are no grounds, moral, practical, or biological, upon which such denial can be justified. Only as women are welcomed into full partnership in all fields of human endeavour will the moral and psychological climate be created in which international peace can emerge.

The cause of universal education, which has already enlisted in its service an army of dedicated people from every faith and nation, deserves the utmost support that the governments of the world can lend it. For ignorance is indisputably the principal reason for the decline and fall of peoples and the perpetuation of prejudice. No nation can achieve success unless education is accorded all its citizens. Lack of resources limits the ability of many nations to fulfil this necessity, imposing a certain ordering of priorities. The decision-making agencies involved would do well to consider giving first priority to the education of women and girls, since it is through educated mothers that the benefits of knowledge can be most effectively and rapidly diffused throughout society. In keeping with the requirements of the times, consideration should also be given to teaching the concept of world citizenship as part of the standard education of every child. *[Universal Education]*

A fundamental lack of communication between peoples seriously undermines efforts towards world peace. Adopting an international auxiliary language would go far to resolving this problem and necessitates the most urgent attention. *[Improved Global Communication]*

Two points bear emphasizing in all these issues. One is that the abolition of war is not simply a matter of signing treaties and protocols; it is a complex task requiring a new level of commitment to resolving issues not customarily associated with the pursuit of peace. Based on political agreements alone, the idea of collective security is a chimera. The other point is that the primary challenge in dealing with issues of peace is to raise the context to the level of principle, as distinct from pure pragmatism. For, in essence, peace stems from an inner state supported by a spiritual or moral attitude, and it is chiefly in evoking this attitude that the possibility of enduring solutions can be found.

There are spiritual principles, or what some call human values, by which solutions can be found for every social problem. Any well-intentioned group can in a general sense devise practical solutions to its problems, but good intentions and practical knowledge are usually not enough. The essential merit of spiritual principle is that it not only presents a perspective which harmonizes with that which is immanent in human nature, it also induces an attitude, a dynamic, a will, an aspiration, which facilitate the discovery and implementation of practical measures. Leaders of governments and all in authority would be well served in their efforts to solve problems if they would first seek to identify the principles involved and then be guided by them.

III

The primary question to be resolved is how the present world, with its entrenched pattern of conflict, can change to a world in which harmony and co-operation will prevail.

World order can be founded only on an unshakeable consciousness of the oneness of mankind, a spiritual truth which all the human sciences confirm. Anthropology, physiology, psychology, recognize only one human species, albeit infinitely varied in the secondary aspects of life.

Unity: The Cardinal Prerequisite for Peace

Recognition of this truth requires abandonment of prejudice—prejudice of every kind—race, class, colour, creed, nation, sex, degree of material civilization, everything which enables people to consider themselves superior to others.

Acceptance of the oneness of mankind is the first fundamental prerequisite for reorganization and administration of the world as one country, the home of humankind. Universal acceptance of this spiritual principle is essential to any successful attempt to establish world peace. It should therefore be universally proclaimed, taught in schools, and constantly asserted in every nation as preparation for the organic change in the structure of society which it implies.

In the Bahá'í view, recognition of the oneness of mankind "calls for no less than the reconstruction and the demilitarization of the whole civilized world—a world organically unified in all the essential aspects of its life, its political machinery, its spiritual aspiration, its trade and finance, its script and language, and yet infinite in the diversity of the national characteristics of its federated units."[10]

Elaborating the implications of this pivotal principle, Shoghi Effendi, the Guardian of the Bahá'í Faith, commented in 1931 that: "Far from aiming at the subversion of the existing foundations of society, it seeks to broaden its basis, to remold its institutions in a manner consonant with the needs of an ever-changing world. It can conflict with no legitimate allegiances, nor can it undermine essential loyalties. Its purpose is neither to stifle the flame of a sane and intelligent patriotism in men's hearts, nor to abolish the system of national autonomy so essential if the evils of excessive centralization are to be avoided. It does not ignore, nor does it attempt to suppress, the diversity of ethnical origins, of climate, of history, of language and tradition, of thought and habit, that differentiate the peoples and nations of the world. It calls for a wider loyalty, for a larger aspiration than any that has animated the human race. It insists upon the subordination of national impulses and interests to the imperative claims of a unified world. It repudiates excessive centralization on one hand, and disclaims all attempts at uniformity on the other. Its watchword is unity in diversity."[11]

The achievement of such ends requires several stages in the adjustment of national political attitudes, which now verge on anarchy in the absence of clearly defined laws or universally accepted and enforceable principles regulating the relationships between nations. The League of Nations, the United Nations, and the many organizations and agreements produced by them have unquestionably been helpful in attenuating some of the negative effects of international conflicts, but they have shown themselves incapable of preventing war. Indeed, there have been scores of wars since the end of the Second World War; many are yet raging.

The predominant aspects of this problem had

Towards a New World Order

already emerged in the nineteenth century when Bahá'u'lláh first advanced his proposals for the establishment of world peace. The principle of collective security was propounded by him in statements addressed to the rulers of the world. Shoghi Effendi commented on his meaning: "What else could these weighty words signify," he wrote, "if they did not point to the inevitable curtailment of unfettered national sovereignty as an indispensable preliminary to the formation of the future Commonwealth of all the nations of the world? Some form of a world super-state must needs be evolved, in whose favour all the nations of the world will have willingly ceded every claim to make war, certain rights to impose taxation and all rights to maintain armaments, except for purposes of maintaining internal order within their respective dominions. Such a state will have to include within its orbit an International Executive adequate to enforce supreme and unchallengeable authority on every recalcitrant member of the commonwealth; a World Parliament whose members shall be elected by the people in their respective countries and whose election shall be confirmed by their respective governments; and a Supreme Tribunal whose judgement will have a binding effect even in such cases where the parties concerned did not voluntarily agree to submit their case to its consideration.

"A world community in which all economic barriers will have been permanently demolished and the interdependence of capital and labour definitely recognized; in which the clamour of religious fanaticism and strife will have been forever stilled; in which the flame of racial animosity will have been finally extinguished; in which a single code of international law—the product of the considered judgement of the world's federated representatives—shall have as its sanction the instant and coercive intervention of the combined forces of the federated units; and finally a world community in which the fury of a capricious and militant nationalism will have been transmuted into an abiding consciousness of world citizenship—such indeed, appears, in its broadest outline, the Order anticipated by Bahá'u'lláh, an Order that shall come to be regarded as the fairest fruit of a slowly maturing age."[12]

The implementation of these far-reaching measures was indicated by Bahá'u'lláh: "The time must come when the imperative necessity for the holding of a vast, an all-embracing assemblage of men will be universally realized. The rulers and kings of the earth must needs attend it, and, participating in its deliberations, must consider such ways and means as will lay the foundations of the world's Great Peace amongst men."[13]

The courage, the resolution, the pure motive, the selfless love of one people for another—all the spiritual and moral qualities required for effecting this momentous step towards peace are focused on the will to act. And it is towards arousing the necessary volition that earnest consideration must be given to the reality of man, namely, his thought. To understand the relevance of this potent reality is also to appreciate the social necessity of actualizing its unique value through candid, dispassionate and cordial consultation, and of acting upon the results of this process. Bahá'u'lláh insistently drew attention to the virtues and indispensability of consultation for ordering human affairs. He said: "Consultation bestows greater awareness and transmutes conjecture into certitude. It is a shining light which, in a dark world, leads the way and guides. For everything there is and will continue to be a station of perfection and maturity. The maturity of the gift of understanding is made manifest through consultation."[14] The very attempt to achieve peace through the consultative action he proposed can release such a salutary spirit among the peoples of the earth that no power could resist the final, triumphal outcome.

Consultation and Conflict Resolution

Concerning the proceedings for this world gathering, 'Abdu'l-Bahá, the son of Bahá'u'lláh and authorized interpreter of his teachings, offered these insights: "They must make the Cause of Peace the object of general consultation, and seek by every means in their power to establish a Union of the nations of the world. They must conclude a binding treaty and establish a covenant, the provisions of which shall be sound, inviolable and definite. They must proclaim it to all the world and obtain for it the sanction of all the human race. This supreme and noble undertaking—the real source of the peace and well-being of all the world—should be regarded as sacred by all that dwell on earth. All the forces of humanity must be mobilized to ensure the stability and permanence of this Most Great Covenant. In this all-embracing Pact the limits and frontiers of each and every nation should be clearly fixed, the principles underlying the relations of governments towards one another definitely laid down, and all international agreements and obligations ascertained. In like manner, the size of the armaments of every government should be strictly limited, for if the preparations for war and the military forces of any nation should be allowed to increase, they will arouse the suspicion of others. The fundamental principle underlying this solemn Pact should be so fixed that if any government later violate any one of its provisions, all the governments on earth should arise to reduce it to utter submission, nay the human race as a whole should resolve, with every power at its disposal, to destroy that government. Should this greatest of all remedies be applied to the sick body of the world, it will assuredly recover from its ills and will remain eternally safe and secure.''[15]

The holding of this mighty convocation is long overdue.

With all the ardour of our hearts, we appeal to the leaders of all nations to seize this opportune moment and take irreversible steps to convoke this world meeting. All the forces of history impel the human race towards this act which will mark for all time the dawn of its long-awaited maturity.

Will not the United Nations, with the full support of its membership, rise to the high purposes of such a crowning event?

Let men and women, youth and children everywhere recognize the eternal merit of this imperative action for all peoples and lift up their voices in willing assent. Indeed, let it be this generation that inaugurates this glorious stage in the evolution of social life on the planet.

IV

The source of the optimism we feel is a vision transcending the cessation of war and the creation of agencies of international co-operation. Permanent peace among nations is an essential stage, but not, Bahá'u'lláh asserts, the ultimate goal of the social development of humanity. Beyond the initial armistice forced upon the world by the fear of nuclear holocaust, beyond the political peace reluctantly entered into by suspicious rival nations, beyond pragmatic arrangements for security and coexistence, beyond even the many experiments in co-operation which these steps will make possible lies the crowning goal: the unification of all the peoples of the world in one universal family.

Disunity is a danger that the nations and peoples of the earth can no longer endure; the consequences are too terrible to contemplate, too obvious to require any demonstration. "The well-being of mankind," Bahá'u'lláh wrote more than a century ago, "its peace and security, are unattainable unless and until its unity is firmly established."[16] In observing that "mankind is groaning, is dying to be led to unity, and to terminate its age-long martyrdom,"[17] Shoghi Effendi further commented that: "Unification of the whole of mankind is the hall-mark of the stage which human society is now approaching. Unity of family, of tribe, of city-state, and nation have been successively attempted and fully established. World unity is the goal towards which a harassed humanity is striving. Nation-building has come to an end. The anarchy inherent in state sovereignty is moving towards a climax. A world, growing to maturity, must abandon this fetish, recognize the oneness and wholeness of human relationships, and establish once and for all the machinery that can best incarnate this fundamental principle of its life."[18]

All contemporary forces of change validate this view. The proofs can be discerned in the many examples already cited of the favourable signs towards world peace in current international movements and developments. The army of men and women, drawn from virtually every culture, race and nation on earth, who serve the multifarious agencies of the United Nations, represent a planetary "civil service" whose impressive accomplishments are indicative of the degree of co-operation that can be attained even under discouraging conditions. An urge towards unity, like a spiritual springtime, struggles to express itself through countless international congresses that bring together people from a vast array of disciplines. It motivates appeals for international projects involving children and youth. Indeed, it is the real source of the remarkable movement towards ecumenism by which members of historically antagonistic religions and sects seem irresistibly drawn towards one another. Together with the opposing tendency to warfare and self-aggrandizement against which it ceaselessly struggles, the drive towards world unity is one of the dominant, pervasive features of life on the planet during the closing years of the twentieth century.

The Experience of the Bahá'í Community

The experience of the Bahá'í community may be seen as an example of this enlarging unity. It is a community of some three to four million people drawn from many nations, cultures, classes and creeds, engaged in a wide range of activities serving the spiritual, social and economic needs of the peoples of many lands. It is a single social organism, representative of the diversity of the human family, conducting its affairs through a system of commonly accepted consultative principles, and cherishing equally all the great outpourings of divine guidance in human history. Its existence is yet another convincing proof of the practicality of its Founder's vision of a united world, another evidence that humanity can live as one global society, equal to whatever challenges its coming of age may entail. If the Bahá'í experience can contribute in whatever measure to reinforcing hope in the unity of the human race, we are happy to offer it as a model for study.

In contemplating the supreme importance of the task now challenging the entire world, we bow our heads in humility before the awesome majesty of the divine Creator, Who out of His infinite love has created all humanity from the same stock; exalted the gem-like reality of man; honoured it with intellect and wisdom, nobility and immortality; and conferred upon man the "unique distinction and capacity to know Him and to love Him," a capacity that "must needs be regarded as the generating impulse and the primary purpose underlying the whole of creation."[19]

We hold firmly the conviction that all human beings have been created "to carry forward an ever-advancing civilization"; that "to act like the beasts of the field is unworthy of man"[20]; that the virtues that befit human dignity are trustworthiness, forbearance, mercy, compassion and loving-kindness towards all peoples. We reaffirm the belief that the "potentialities inherent in the station of man, the full measure of his destiny on earth, the innate excellence of his reality, must all be manifested in this promised Day of God."[21] These are the motivations for our unshakeable faith that unity and peace are the attainable goal towards which humanity is striving.

At this writing, the expectant voices of Bahá'ís can be heard despite the persecution they still endure in the land in which their Faith was born. By their example of steadfast hope, they bear witness to the belief that the imminent realization of this age-old dream of peace is now, by virtue of the transforming effects of Bahá'u'lláh's revelation, invested with the force of divine authority. Thus we convey to you not only a vision in words: we summon the power of deeds of faith and sacrifice; we convey the anxious plea of our co-religionists everywhere for peace and unity. We join with all who are the victims of aggression, all who yearn for an end to conflict and contention, all whose devotion to principles of peace and world order promotes the ennobling purposes for which humanity was called into being by an all-loving Creator.

In the earnestness of our desire to impart to you the fervour of our hope and the depth of our confidence, we cite the emphatic promise of Bahá'u'lláh: "These fruitless strifes, these ruinous wars shall pass away, and the 'Most Great Peace' shall come."[22]

UNIVERSAL HOUSE OF JUSTICE

Notes

1. Pierre Teilhard de Chardin, *The Future of Man*, trans. Norman Denny (London: William Collins and Son, 1964), 129.
2. Bahá'u'lláh, *Tablets of Bahá'u'lláh* (Haifa, Israel: Bahá'í World Centre, 1978), 171.
3. Bahá'u'lláh, *Gleanings from the Writings of Bahá'u'lláh*, 3rd ed. (Wilmette, Illinois: Bahá'í Publishing Trust, 1976), 340.
4. Arnold Toynbee, Preface to *Religion in a Secular Age: The Search for Final Meaning* by John Cogley (London: Pall Mall Press, 1968), p. viii. The full context of the statement can be seen in the following passage: "If the definition of religion as a total concern about Man's World is correct, it follows that in any human society—even the least closely integrated ones—religion will enter into all human affairs. Religion is a faculty of human nature, and human nature has its roots in nature."
5. Bahá'u'lláh, cited in *The World Order of Bahá'u'lláh*, Shoghi Effendi, 2nd ed. (Wilmette, Illinois: Bahá'í Publishing Trust, 1974), 186.
6. Bahá'u'lláh, *Tablets of Bahá'u'lláh*, 125.
7. Shoghi Effendi, *The World Order of Bahá'u'lláh*, 187.
8. Shoghi Effendi, *The World Order of Bahá'u'lláh*, 42.
9. Bahá'u'lláh, *Tablets of Bahá'u'lláh*, 167.
10. Shoghi Effendi, *The World Order of Bahá'u'lláh*, 43.
11. Shoghi Effendi, *The World Order of Bahá'u'lláh*, 41–42.
12. Shoghi Effendi, *The World Order of Bahá'u'lláh*, 40–41.
13. Bahá'u'lláh, *Gleanings*, 249.
14. *Consultation: A Compilation, Extracts from the Writings and Utterances of Bahá'u'lláh, 'Abdu'l-Bahá, Shoghi Effendi and the Universal House of Justice* (Toronto: Bahá'í Community of Canada, 1980), 3.
15. 'Abdu'l-Bahá, cited in *The World Order of Bahá'u'lláh*, 37–38.
16. Bahá'u'lláh, *Gleanings*, 286.
17. Shoghi Effendi, *The World Order of Bahá'u'lláh*, 201.
18. Shoghi Effendi, *The World Order of Bahá'u'lláh*, 202.
19. Bahá'u'lláh, *Gleanings*, 65.
20. Bahá'u'lláh, *Gleanings*, 215.
21. Bahá'u'lláh, *Gleanings*, 340.
22. Bahá'u'lláh, cited in *The Promised Day Is Come*, Shoghi Effendi, 3rd ed. (Wilmette, Illinois: Bahá'í Publishing Trust, 1980), 116.

Part Two
Annotations

The Quest for Peace

"The Great Peace towards which people of good will throughout the centuries have inclined their hearts, of which seers and poets for countless generations have expressed their vision, and for which from age to age the sacred scriptures of mankind have constantly held the promise...."

". . . and they shall beat their swords into plowshares, and their spears into pruninghooks: nation shall not lift up sword against nation, neither shall they learn war any more."
Isaiah, 2:4 (repeated in Micah 4:3).

□

"Depart from evil, and do good; seek peace, and pursue it."
Psalms 34:14.

□

"Weapons, however ornamental, are not a source of happiness, but are dreaded by all. Therefore the man of Tao will not abide where such things are...."
Lao Tse (c. 570–490 B.C.), *Tao-Teh-King*.

□

"Let us therefore now do good. What can we do that is good? Let us now abstain from taking life. That is a good thing that we may take up and do. And they will abstain from slaughter, and will continue in this good way....

"Among such humans, brethren, at Ketumati the royal city, there will arise Sankha, a Wheel-turning king, righteous and ruling in righteousness... He will live in supremacy over this earth to its ocean bounds, having conquered it not by the scourge, not by the sword, but by righteousness."
Buddha (c. 560–480 B.C.), *Dialogues of the Buddha*.

□

"Peace, with justice and honour, is the fairest and most profitable of

possessions."
  Polybius (c. 204–122 B.C.), *Histories* 4:31.

☐

"I prefer the most unfair peace to the most righteous war."
  Cicero (106–43 B.C.), *Epistola ad Atticum*.

☐

"Fair peace is becoming to men; fierce anger belongs to beasts."
  Ovid (43 B.C.–A.D. 18), *Ars Amatoria*.

☐

"Blessed are the peacemakers: for they shall be called the children of God."
  Matthew 5:9.

☐

"The disciples of the wise increase peace in the world."
  Talmud, Berakoth 64a.

☐

"The believers are but a single Brotherhood: so make peace and reconciliation between your two (contending) brothers; and fear Allah, that ye may receive mercy."
  Qur'an 49, 10.

☐

"Amidst the calm and tranquility of peace the human race accomplishes most freely and easily its given work...whence it is manifest that universal peace is the best of those things that are ordained for our beatitude."
  Dante Alighieri (1265–1321), *De Monarchia* 1, 4.

☐

"The most disadvantageous peace is better than the most just war."
  Erasmus (1466–1536), *Adagia*.

☐

I am Deganawidah and with the chiefs of the Five Nations
I plant the Tree of the Great Peace...
If any man of any nation
Shall desire to obey the laws of the Great Peace
He may trace the roots to their source and be welcome
To shelter beneath the Great Peace...

I Deganawidah
And the chiefs of our Five Nations of the Great Peace

> We now uproot the tallest pine
> into the cavity thereby made
> we cast all weapons
> Into the depths of the earth
> Into the deep underneath...
> We cast all weapons of war
> We bury them from sight forever...
> And we plant again the tree...
> Thus shall the Great Peace be established.
>
> Iroquois poem, "The Tree of the Great Peace." Cited in *Peace on Earth: A Peace Anthology* (Paris: UNESCO, 1980), 34–35.

☐

"... nature guarantees the coming of perpetual peace, through the natural course of human propensities: not indeed with sufficient certainty to enable us to prophesy the future of this ideal theoretically, but yet clearly enough for practical purposes. And thus this guarantee of nature makes it a duty that we should labour for this end, an end which is no mere chimera... and since peace cannot be effected or guaranteed without a compact among nations, they must form an alliance of a peculiar kind, which may be called a pacific alliance (*foedus pacificum*), different from a treaty of peace (*pactum pacis*), inasmuch as it would forever terminate all wars, whereas the latter only ends one."
   I. Kant (1724–1804), *Perpetual Peace*.

☐

"Sooner or later mankind must come to one universal peace, unless our race is to be destroyed by the increasing power of its own destructive inventions; and that universal peace must needs take the form of a government, that is to say, a law-sustaining organization, in the best sense of the word religious—a government ruling men through the educated co-ordination of their minds in a common conception of human history and human destiny."
   H.G. Wells (1866–1946), *Crux Ansata*.

☐

"Peace cannot be kept by force. It can only be achieved by understanding."
   A. Einstein (1879–1955), *Notes on Pacifism*.

☐

"If we value our own lives, and the lives of our children and all children everywhere, if we honour both the past and the future, then we must do everything in our power to work non-violently for Peace."
   Margaret Laurence, quoted in *Canadian Woman Studies* (6: 1), 122.

"We are so convinced that Peace is the goal of mankind in the process of its growing self-awareness and of the development of society on the face of the earth, that today, for the new year and for future years, we dare to proclaim, as we did last year: Peace is possible. . . .
"Peace is possible only if it is considered a duty. . . Peace must take hold of the conscience of men as a supreme ethical objective. . . Peace is above all an idea . . . humanity must be at Peace, that is, united and consistent in itself. . . .
"Peace is possible, if each one of us wants it; if each one of us loves Peace. . . defends Peace, works for Peace. Each one of us must listen to his own conscience to the impelling call: 'Peace depends on you too.'"
Pope Paul VI (1897–1978), *Peace Depends on You Too.*

☐

". . . may peace reign on earth, and may the gourd and the pot agree. May their animals live in harmony and all evil speech be banished into the bush and the virgin forest."
A prayer from Guinea. Cited in *Peace on Earth*, 35.

☐

"More than an end to war, we want an end to the beginnings of all wars."
Franklin D. Roosevelt

☐

"All the works of love are works of peace. . . . We do not need bombs and guns; We need love and compassion. . . . If everyone could see the image of God in his neighbour, do you think we should still need tanks and generals?"
Mother Teresa, "A Meeting of the World Conference of Religion for Peace," *Youth Corps Magazine*, 1982.

☐

"What nobler theme than the 'good of the world and the happiness of the nations' can occupy our lives? The message of universal peace will surely prevail. It is useless to combine or conspire against an idea which has in it potency to create a new earth and a new heaven and to quicken human beings with a holy passion of service."
Helen Keller. Quoted in *The Bahá'í World* 11 (1946–1950) (Wilmette, Illinois: Bahá'í Publishing Committee, 1952), 454.

☐

"On the contrary, thanks to the unfailing grace of God, the lovingkindness of His favored ones, the unrivaled endeavors of wise and capable souls, and the thoughts and ideas of the peerless leaders of this age, nothing whatsoever can be regarded as unattainable. Many a cause which past ages have regarded as purely visionary, yet in this day has become most easy and practicable. Why should this most great and lofty Cause—the day-star of the firmament of true civilization and the cause of the glory, the advancement, the well-being and the success of all humanity—be regarded as impossible of achievement?"

'Abdu'l-Bahá, *The Secret of Divine Civilization*, 2nd ed. (Wilmette, Illinois: Bahá'í Publishing Trust, 1970), 66.

Technology:
For War or Peace?

"*The scientific and technological advances occurring in this unusually blessed century portend a great surge forward in the social evolution of the planet, and indicate the means by which the practical problems of humanity may be solved.... Yet barriers persist.*"

"Man has made tremendous strides in the area of technology in this century. We now have everything from space-flight to insulin, from computers to lasers, and from communications satellites to inoculations for dozens of diseases that were once major killers. Nevertheless, societies have chosen to devote much of their technology to the area of war. What is needed is a major shift in priorities which would further the search for a technology of peace.

Consider that in 1983 the world's military bill was close to U.S. $800 billion.

1) A half day's military expenditures would finance the whole malaria eradication program of the World Health Organization.
2) The price of a modern tank—at least $1 million—could improve storage facilities for 100,000 tons of rice and thus save 4,000 tons or more annually. One person can live on little more than a pound of rice a day. The same expenditure could buy 1,000 classrooms for 30,000 children.
3) The cost of one jet fighter—$20 million—would pay for about 40,000 village pharmacies.
4) One-half of 1 per cent of a single year's military expenditure would pay for the farm equipment needed to increase food production and provide near self-sufficiency in all food-deficit, low-income countries by 1990."

W. Brandt, "The North-South Challenge," *World Press Review* 31: 6 (June 1984), 22–23.

□

"One of the most puzzling aspects of the scientific and technological progress of humanity is the fact that much of man's scientific activities and technology are used in the service of war. In 1978, 20 billion dollars were spent on finding 'new ways to kill man.' And some of this amount went to pay 500,000 scientists who are diligently searching for more sophisticated methods to kill. This dedication to the creation of the technology of war is primarily due to two misconceptions: the misconception about the true nature of man and the misconception about the true nature of the relationship between science and religion....

"If the human soul is not guided by spiritual, moral, and ethical precepts, then it becomes solely preoccupied with the material side of life and creates conditions most suitable for the development of the technology of war....

"This is the condition of our world today. Many governments and scientists are engaged in activities which cause evil, hurt, and destruction. These are the conditions which impelled Aurelio Peccei, in 1974, to observe:

Our nations, instead of uniting in a supreme effort, are still egocentric and antagonistic with each other and busy arming and trading in all sorts of weapons. You know that the nuclear stock piles, already in existence, pack so much explosive that they can wipe out mankind in a few hours. Each one of us has, in those stockpiles, an endowment of TNT or ordinary explosives equal to 12 tons. This is sheer madness. But it is only the reflection of the moral disorder and disintegration of a society which invests, every year, some of its best scientific and political energies and between 6 and 8 percent of the total world product in perfecting the doctrines, the technologies, the armament of extermination. This is a society in which the tragic irony exists that we trust security in what, using a trade word in defence circles, is called M.A.D. (mad, mutual assured destruction).

"The human rational soul, however, once enlightened by the spiritual teachings, can reconcile the supposedly irreconcilable realities of science and religion and create a new technology of peace. In order to comprehend better the concept of such a technology, we must return to the issue of man's spiritual nature.

". . . the fundamental faculties of the soul are knowledge, love, and will. These three faculties, although non-physical in essence, are nevertheless dependent upon physical instruments to manifest themselves in this life. Thus, a thought or an idea can be transmitted only through physical faculties and instruments such as speaking, writing, and visual demonstrations, and tactile and other sensory modalities. Likewise, love is shown through the faculties of touch, sight, speech, cooperative activities, and a host of other processes, all of which are dependent upon the use of the body. The same is true of human will.

"In addition, man invents instruments and objects to extend and even surpass the potential of different parts of his body. Thus, man, through the power of his soul, creates machines which allow him to fly, to move quickly, to handle the most minute objects and to perform other physical feats which would be otherwise not in the capacity of his body. For example, man, with the help of his knowledge and his power of understanding, not only sees and studies objects with his eyes, but expands the capacity of his eyes by inventing the microscope, the telescope, the television, satellites, and other instruments that allow the human soul to see ever deeper, farther and more clearly. The same is true with inventions which broaden the scope of human capacity for hearing, touch, smell and taste.

"However, of all man's inventions, the most interesting and significant are those inventions which facilitate and extend the work of his brain, which is the seat and the main instrument of his soul. Here I am referring to all machines and instruments which perform mathematical and logical functions hitherto performed by only the most educated people. The computer is an extension of the human brain and is, therefore, another very important accessory to the human body, which, as a whole, functions as a tool for the human soul. It would be a folly, a mistake of immense gravity, if we were to see machines and other human inventions as anything but extensions of the physical reality of man, which, in turn, is meaningful and alive only if it is quickened, influenced, and directed by the human power of understanding, which is the human soul. If man decides, through the perversity of his own self, to abdicate his power and control over to his inventions, then he decreases the world of life to a world of mechanistic, meaningless, and destructive movement, the movement of machines."

    H. Danesh, *Unity: The Creative Foundation for Peace.* Scheduled for publication Spring, 1986, by the Association for Bahá'í Studies. Citation of Aurelio Peccei from *Dilemmas of Modern Man* (Winnipeg, Can.: Great West Life Assurance Co., 1975), 19.

☐

"In other words, it is the whole question of developing proper social mechanisms for the responsible implementation of new technologies that needs to be addressed, and not just the particular question of applications of current nuclear technology. If the problem of the implementation of each new technology is treated in an *ad hoc* fashion, with a view towards either avoiding public discussion or provoking public reaction through strong condemnatory statements, the public will eventually become mistrustful and insensitive. The fact that the public has remained largely unaware of the considerable in-depth discussion of moral and ethical issues that has already taken place within industry and government has important consequences for public opinion."

    Bahá'í Community of Canada, Submission to the Interfaith Program for Public Awareness of Nuclear Issues, November 1, 1984.

The Spectre of War

"Flaws in the prevailing order are conspicuous in the inability of sovereign states organized as United Nations to exorcize the spectre of war. . . ."

In 1983 alone, some 45 nations or 1/4 of all the world's countries were experiencing war of some sort. The bloodiest of those conflicts included the following:

Cambodia/Kampuchea: Civil War and Foreign Invasion. Dead since 1970: 4 million
Indonesia: Guerrilla war. Dead since 1975: 100,000–250,000
Lebanon: Civil war. Dead since 1975: 85,000
Afghanistan: Civil war. Dead since 1978: 100,000
Iran-Iraq. Conventional war. Dead since 1980: 100,000
Philippines: Guerrilla wars. Dead since 1972: 50,000
Vietnam-China: Conventional war. Dead since 1979: 47,000
El Salvador: Guerrilla war. Dead since 1977: over 30,000
Guatemala: Guerrilla war. Dead since 1982: 12,000–22,000
Ethiopia: Guerrilla war. Dead since 1962: 30,000
  U.S. News and World Report (March 28, 1983), 11.

□

". . . since the Second World War, 199 wars have been fought in the world, 350 years have been spent on fighting them, 69 countries have been directly the theatre of a war, and no fewer than 81 countries have been directly or indirectly involved in these war conflicts since 1945."
  Janez Stanovnik, "The Debit Balance of the Mistakes of Several Decades" in *What Kind of a World Are We Leaving Our Children?* (Paris: UNESCO, 1978), 73.

□

The toll from these evils in this century alone is enormous. World War One caused the deaths of some 8 ½ million soldiers and some 5 million civilians. World War Two created even greater destruction with death tolls estimated at between 35 and 60 million.

In the Iran-Iraq war, the struggle has intensified so much that by fall 1984 over 250,000 deaths have been reported.
[Editor's note]

☐

"Gil Elliot made a valiant effort to count 'the number of man-made deaths in the twentieth century.' He arrived at a total of 110 million, which he regards as 'a reasonably conservative estimate '.... The 110 million fatalities (from 1900 to 1970) include 38 million soldiers. Since these losses result from war and civil war, they cannot properly be attributed to crimes against humanity (in a legal sense)....To repeat, those are conservative estimates and it is entirely possible, even probable, that deliberate crimes against humanity cost the lives of substantially more than 100 million. That means that during the twentieth century, one out of every 30 inhabitants of the earth was killed through government criminality....This does not include the toll exacted by private criminals, routine crime-fighting by the police, and legitimate death penalties."
K. Glaser and S.T. Possony, *Victims of Politics: The State and Human Rights* (New York: Columbia University Press, 1979), 43–44.

Aggression and Human Nature

"Indeed, so much have aggression and conflict come to characterize our social, economic and religious systems, that many have succumbed to the view that such behaviour is intrinsic to human nature and therefore ineradicable."

"A number of views of the nature of man are currently advanced, some of them quite contradictory, and most of them failing to alleviate the ongoing destructiveness of contemporary life because they do not take into account man's spiritual as well as his material nature.
"Floyd W. Watson, in *The Idea of Man,* says:
   If it is true, in general, that "ideas have consequences," then man's ideas about man have the most far-reaching consequences of all. Upon them may depend the structure of government, the patterns of culture, the purpose of education, the design of the future and the human or inhuman uses of human beings.
"Watson goes on to describe the major prevailing ideas of the nature of man, giving three models: man as beast, man as machine, and man as 'a free agent—a creative actor on the world stage.'
"In the early decades of this century, whose wars have made anything experienced by previous decades seem insignificant, Freud postulated that man had been created at the mercy of his instincts, which were seen to be essentially of two kinds: life and death, love and hatred (i.e., the sexual and the aggressive instincts). Elaborating on this theory, he wrote that human instincts are 'only of two kinds: those which seek to preserve and unite, and those which seek to destroy and kill.'
"The discouraging view of aggression that Freud cast upon psychological thought is still less pessimistic than that of Lorenz and other ethologists. Gorney observes that, to Lorenz, love is nothing but made-over aggression, and that the elimination of aggression would also eliminate love."
   H. Danesh, "The Violence-Free Society," *Bahá'í Studies* (October, 1979), 3. Citation of Floyd W. Watson from *The Idea of Man* (New York: Delacorte Press, 1976), 11–12.

"If it were truly the case that the human animal is unswervingly propelled toward open conflict with members of its own species, then the prospects for long-term tenure of technological society on earth would be very poor indeed. With the means of mass destruction at hand, it would be merely a matter of time before their use dealt a blow to life on earth from which it might never recover. Those who argue that humans are innately aggressive must therefore be pointing to the inevitability of such an event.

Unfortunately, it does not necessarily follow that a humanity not harboring inbuilt aggressiveness will avoid reaching the same end, as our recent history and current political posturing so clearly warns us. The possibility of a massive international confrontation is real. . . .

"Primates, particularly the higher primates, are all social animals: they live in groups and engage in complex social interactions. It is, therefore, not surprising that, as primates, humans too are social animals. But unlike any other primates we extend social behavior into the patterns of subsistence. The core of human evolution was the social group focused on a food-sharing economy: plant foods and meat were brought to a home base and shared. Without a keenly developed sense of cooperation the social organization needed for day-to-day division of activities between members of the group, which is the basis of the mixed economy, could not have worked.

"Because the mixed economy of hunting and gathering brings with it a much more efficient exploitation of resources in the environment and also sharpens the edge of social interactions—both of which enhance adaptability of the human animal—evolutionary forces favored its development. It is probably the single most important factor in the emergence of mankind. And cooperation was an essential element of its success. More than any other piece of social behavior, the motivation to cooperate in group effort is a direct legacy of the nature of human evolution.

"To insist that blind cooperation is a universal aspect of human behavior would, of course, be to negate the flexibility and independence of the human mind. What is in us is a very readily-tapped tendency for group identification and group endeavor. Most communities have social rules and customs (the stuff of culture) that provide a framework through which 'groupness' is expressed. The rules and customs of different communities may vary, and ethnic groups may express their identification through such material channels as self-decoration or domestic architecture. But, throughout, the goal is the same: the sense of belonging to and therefore contributing to the group. We all experience such an urge, and it may extend from the need to be 'accepted' by a group as small as perhaps three or four people at school, in college, or within the local community, all the way to supporting a national sports team along with tens of thousands of other fans."
      Richard E. Leakey and Roger Lewin, *Origins: What New Discoveries Reveal About the Emergence of Our Species and its Possible Future*

(New York: E.P. Dutton, 1977), 244–248.

☐

"... in *The Anatomy of Human Destructiveness*, Erich Fromm reviews the evidence against the instinctiveness thesis and reaches the conclusion that data from the neurosciences, animal behaviour studies and the fields of paleontology and anthropology indicate that the instinctiveness interpretation of human destructiveness is not tenable. Eron and associates, through a 10-year longitudinal study, concluded that aggressive behaviour is shaped by learning through socialization practices.

"Still others consider violence to be the result of both instinctual and educational forces. However, in spite of obvious differences between these various groups regarding the roots of violence, they all view man as an animal.

"The notion of man as a biochemical machine also has strong supporters and is well-accepted in many scientific and ideological circles. Such a view considers all human activities to be a reaction to a specific stimulus. As such, human beings are perceived to be amenable to manipulation in the same manner that computers and robots respond to programming. Robots, however, are merely well-programmed machines, and, like animals, who act on instincts of aggression, competition and territoriality, are unable to make conscious moral choices or distinguish between right and wrong.

"Still another notion of man considers him to be essentially sinful, and utilizes guilt and shame as the main motivating forces in shaping his life processes. Like the other views mentioned it also has the quality of degrading man, and either justifying his most primitive and animal-like emotions and actions, or creating a state of conflict and despair in him.

"The Bahá'í teachings regarding the nature of man, on the other hand, clearly state that man possesses both a spiritual and material nature. 'Abdu'l-Bahá elaborates upon this:

> In man there are two natures; his spiritual or higher nature and his material or lower nature. In one he approaches God, in the other he lives for the world alone. Signs of both these natures are to be found in men. In his material aspect he expresses untruth, cruelty and injustice; all these are the outcome of his lower nature. The attributes of his divine nature are shown forth in love, mercy, kindness, truth and justice. . . .

"For the individual to acquire these spiritual qualities, he needs to be illuminated and guided by the divine spirit which reaches him through the teachings of the Manifestation of God for his age. If the individual allows his rational soul and his power of understanding to receive this spiritual illumination and guidance, his sublime spiritual nature will manifest itself. On the other hand, if he doesn't use or develop his spiritual qualities, '. . . they become atrophied, enfeebled and at last incapable.' The outcome of such a process is that the material qualities of man take ascendance and consequently '. . . the unhappy, misguided man becomes more savage, more unjust, more vile, more cruel, more malevolent than the lower animals themselves.'

"It is this all-encompassing and spiritual education which helps the individual become aware of his essential nobility and learn to safeguard it."

H. Danesh, "The Violence-Free Society," *Bahá'í Studies* (October, 1979), 3–5. Citation of 'Abdu'l-Bahá from *Paris Talks*, 11th ed. (London: Bahá'í Publishing Trust, 1971), 60.

Collective Growth of Mankind

"The Bahá'í Faith regards the current world confusion and calamitous condition in human affairs as a natural phase in an organic process leading ultimately and irresistibly to the unification of the human race in a single social order whose boundaries are those of the planet."

"Bahá'u'lláh teaches that mankind as a whole experiences stages of growth and development similar to those experienced by individual human beings. Thus, at one time, mankind collectively was in its infancy, at another time, in its childhood, and now is going through a period of adolescence, rapidly approaching its maturity. Shoghi Effendi, in referring to this growth process, describes the present state of mankind in the following manner:

> The long ages of infancy and childhood, through which the human race had to pass, have receded into the background. Humanity is now experiencing the commotions invariably associated with the most turbulent stage of its evolution, the stage of adolescence, when the impetuosity of youth and its vehemence reach their climax, and must gradually be superseded by the calmness, the wisdom and the maturity that characterize the stage of manhood. Then will the human race reach that stature of ripeness which will enable it to acquire all the powers and capacities upon which its ultimate development must depend.

"Adolescence is a period of rapid change, of upheavals and confusion. The adolescent needs an appropriate environment in which he can sail through this turbulent stage and arrive at the calm shores of adulthood. If the adolescent is not provided with such an environment, his very integrity is threatened and conflicts arise. Emotions and passions take charge of him and, in his lonely and misguided struggle, he succumbs to destruction, violence or apathy.

"Mankind, now in its adolescence, is gradually realizing that it is incapable of directing its own growth alone, and is slowly becoming aware that a total change in the thinking, life-style, attitudes, beliefs and consciousness of humanity must precede any improvement in its present

dilemma."
H. Danesh, "The Violence-Free Society," 22. Citation of Shoghi Effendi from *The World Order of Bahá'u'lláh*, 202.

☐

"Because the establishment of world unity and a planetary civilization represents the consummation of mankind's development on this planet, it represents the 'coming of age' of humanity, the maturity of the human race. Shoghi Effendi expressed this idea as follows:
The Revelation of Bahá'u'lláh, whose supreme mission is none other than the achievement of this organic and spiritual unity of the whole body of nations, should, if we be faithful to its implications, be regarded as signalizing through its advent the *coming of age of the entire human race*. It should be viewed . . . as marking the last and highest stage in the stupendous evolution of man's collective life on this planet. The emergence of a world community, the consciousness of world citizenship, the founding of a world civilization and culture . . . should, by their very nature, be regarded, as far as this planetary life is concerned, as the furthermost limits in the organization of human society, though man, as an individual, will, nay must indeed as a result of such a consummation, continue indefinitely to progress and develop.

"The different stages in mankind's development are regarded as quite similar to the stages in the life of the individual. The current stage is described as that of adolescence, the stage immediately preceding full maturity. . .
That mystic, all-pervasive, yet indefinable change, which we associate with the stage of maturity inevitable in the life of the individual . . . must . . . have its counterpart in the evolution of the organization of human society. A similar stage must sooner or later be attained in the collective life of mankind, producing an even more striking phenomenon in world relations, and endowing the whole human race with such potentialities of well-being as shall provide, throughout the succeeding ages, the chief incentive required for the eventual fulfillment of its high destiny."
W. Hatcher and J.D. Martin, *The Bahá'í Faith: The Emerging Global Religion* (New York: Harper and Row, 1984), 79-80. Citations of Shoghi Effendi from *The World Order of Bahá'u'lláh*, 163-164.

The Transcendent Nature of the Human Spirit

"The endowments which distinguish the human race from all other forms of life are summed up in what is known as the human spirit; the mind is its essential quality. These endowments have enabled humanity to build civilizations and to prosper materially. But such accomplishments alone have never satisfied the human spirit, whose mysterious nature inclines it towards transcendence, a reaching toward an invisible realm, towards the ultimate reality, that unknowable essence of essences called God."

"There is within each of us a potential for goodness beyond our imagining; for giving which seeks no reward; for listening without judgement; for loving unconditionally.

"It is our goal to reach that potential. We can approach it, in ways large and small every minute of every day, if we try.

"When we have found that path, we have built our own 'home of peace' inside of ourselves."

Dr. Elizabeth Kubler-Ross, *Working It Through* (New York: Mac-Millan Publishers, 1982), 29.

☐

"Bahá'u'lláh described God's purpose for man in the following way:
 The purpose of God in creating man hath been, and will ever be, to enable him to know his Creator and to attain His Presence. To this most excellent aim, this supreme objective, all the heavenly and the divinely-revealed and weighty Scriptures unequivocally bear witness.

"Life should be seen as an eternal process of joyous spiritual discovery and growth: in the beginning stages of earthly life, the individual undergoes a period of training and education which, if it is successful, gives him the basic intellectual and spiritual tools necessary for continued growth. When one attains physical maturity in adulthood, he becomes responsible for his further progress, which now depends entirely on the efforts he himself makes. Through the daily struggles of material existence, one gradually deepens his understanding of the spiritual principles underlying reality, and this understanding enables him to relate more effectively to himself, to others, and to God. After physical death, the individual continues to grow and develop in the spiritual world, which is greater than the physical world, just as the physical world is greater than the world we inhabit while in our mother's womb.

"This last statement is based on the Bahá'í concept of the soul and of life after physical death. According to the Bahá'í teachings, man's true nature is spiritual. Beyond the physical body, each human being has a rational soul, created by God. This soul is a nonmaterial entity, which does not depend on the body. Rather the body serves as its vehicle in the physical world. The soul of an individual comes into being at the moment the physical body is conceived and continues to exist after the death of the physical body. The soul (also called the spirit) of the individual is the seat or locus of his personality, self, and consciousness.

"The evolution or development of the soul and its capacities is the basic purpose of human existence. This evolution is towards God and its motive force is knowledge of God and love for Him. As we learn about God, our love for him increases; and this, in turn, enables us to attain a closer communication with our Creator. Also, as we draw closer to God, our character becomes more refined and our actions reflect more and more the attributes and qualities of God....

"The Bahá'í writings refer to the gradual evolution or development of the individual soul as 'spiritual progress'. 'Spiritual progress' means acquiring the capacity to act in conformity with the Will of God and to express the attributes and spirit of God in one's dealings with one's self and with other human beings. Bahá'u'lláh teaches that the only true and enduring happiness for man lies in the pursuit of spiritual development."
    Hatcher/Martin, *The Bahá'í Faith*, 100–101. Citation of Bahá'u'lláh from *Gleanings*, 70.

☐

"... how difficult it is so to dismiss the universe, our world, the animal, and vegetable world, and man. How clearly one sees a plan in everything. How unthinkable it is that the miraculous development that has brought man's body, brain and spirit to what it is, should cease. Why would it cease?

"Not the body, which is only an instrument, but the invisible spark or fire within the body which makes man one with the wider creation."
    Queen Marie of Rumania from a letter appearing in the *Toronto Daily Star* (September 28, 1926). Quoted in *The Bahá'í World* 11 (1946–1950), 427.

Progressive Revelation

"The religions brought to mankind by a succession of spiritual luminaries have been the primary link between humanity and that ultimate reality [God], and have galvanized and refined mankind's capacity to achieve spiritual success together with social progress."

In its statement addressed to the peoples of the world, the Universal House of Justice makes use of a number of terms, such as "spiritual luminaries," "Educators," "Founders," and "Prophets of God" which refer to the Bahá'í concept of the Manifestations of God, and which in turn relate to the theme of the Progressive Revelation of the religions of mankind.

□

"The Revelation proclaimed by Bahá'u'lláh, His followers believe, is divine in origin, all-embracing in scope, broad in its outlook, scientific in its method, humanitarian in its principles and dynamic in the influence it exerts on the hearts and minds of men. The mission of the Founder of their Faith, they conceive. . . to be to proclaim that religious truth is not absolute but relative, that Divine Revelation is continuous and progressive, that the Founders of all past religions, though different in the non-essential aspects of their teachings, 'abide in the same Tabernacle, soar in the same heaven, are seated upon the same throne, utter the same speech and proclaim the same Faith.' His Cause, they have already demonstrated, stands identified with, and revolves around, the principle of the organic unity of mankind as representing the consummation of the whole process of human evolution. This final stage in this stupendous evolution, they assert, is not only necessary but inevitable, that it is gradually approaching, and that nothing short of the celestial potency with which a divinely ordained Message can claim to be endowed can succeed in establishing it."

Shoghi Effendi, *Selected Writings of Shoghi Effendi* (Wilmette, Ill: Bahá'í Publishing Trust, 1975), 1.

"Seen in perspective, there is nothing unnatural about the appearance of these Educators. They come forward as part of what might be called a spiritual law, in response to the needs of society, at times of great moral confusion and despair which occur with the decline of established beliefs or because new circumstances have arisen for which traditional answers are no longer suitable. Phrased in another way, these flashes of light occur when society reaches a point of explosion, just as in nature, at critical points, a solid will turn into liquid, a liquid into gas, a seed will burst into a plant, a chrysalis into a butterfly.

"The Educators are the Founders of the great religions. Many lived before recorded history; others have come to societies who have lost much of their record of the past. Those Whom we do have some knowledge of are Abraham, Moses, Krishna, Buddha, Zoroaster, Jesus, Muhammad, and now the Báb and Bahá'u'lláh.

"Bahá'í Writings distinguish two aspects to the teachings of these Educators. First, they all have in common the same universal themes which must govern man's attitude toward God, his fellowmen and the universe at large: love, justice, detachment from personal desire, honesty, selflessness, faithfulness, humility, forgiveness, charity, obedience, mercy, trustworthiness, sincerity, truthfulness, moderation. These truths are not just words. When society forgets them, the resulting pain is sharp and deep. Secondly, each includes social teachings appropriate to the level of development of the society existing at the time. . . .

"Not only did the Educators recognize Their Predecessors but They have also had the vision to see that the need would continue. In Their teachings They would refer to Their own return, not as a bodily reincarnation as some have mistakenly believed, but in the spirit. . . .

"This theme is of the utmost importance in providing a basis for the unity of mankind. It means that men of all religions may have a common belief concerning the most significant aspects of existence, without having to deny the essence of their previous belief. If men were to remain divided on questions concerning their deepest feelings and beliefs then there could be no true brotherhood, at best a fragile tolerance based on indifference. The theme is also of considerable significance for those who have in the past turned against religion, because it shows that when religion is truly practised it is not exclusive, narrow, and a source of incessant quarrelling but the instrument for establishing mutual understanding and appreciation between all men."

John Huddleston, *The Earth Is but One Country* (London: Bahá'í Publishing Trust, 1976), 36–39.

☐

"How often in the past the divinely revealed Laws have set in motion social trends destined to completely reshape the affairs of men. Who shall dare to limit the effect of the ten commandments of Moses? Who can deny the effect of the Laws of Jesus? Who can fail to see the rise of the

Arabic people in the middle ages, following the proclamation of Muhammad's Law? Every stability we claim must acknowledge as its source the coming of Divine Law to a people."

Dorothy Baker, "The Most Great Peace," *The Bahá'í World* 10 (1944–1946), 656–657.

Role of Religion in Achieving World Peace

"Writing of religion as a social force, Bahá'u'lláh said: 'Religion is the greatest of all means for the establishment of order in the world and for the peaceful contentment of all that dwell therein.'"

"The fundamental purpose animating the Faith of God and His Religion is to safeguard the interests and promote the unity of the human race, and to foster the spirit of love and fellowship amongst men. Suffer it not to become a source of dissension and discord, of hate and enmity."
Bahá'u'lláh, *Gleanings from the Writings of Bahá'u'lláh*, 215.

☐

"Religion is verily the chief instrument for the establishment of order in the world and of tranquillity amongst its peoples."
Bahá'u'lláh, *Tablets of Bahá'u'lláh*, 63–64.

☐

"The religion of God is for love and unity; make it not the cause of enmity and dissension."
Bahá'u'lláh, *Tablets of Bahá'u'lláh*, p. 220.

☐

"Even as the love of God gives a man new values with which to measure other men and his relationship with them, it also gives him a deeper regard for the law and order which are the basis for any progressive society. Loyalty to spiritual principle and conscientious use of it in human affairs is the beginning of social order and security. The spiritual laws of God give men his great ethical standards. Belief in God and sincere effort to live one's faith are the generative forces of man's conscience. When human conscience and social ethics are united in their objectives there is cooperation between inner and outer disciplines. The result is a matured and refined individual and society."
Elsie Austin, "World Unity as a Way of Life," *The Bahá'í World* 11 (1946–1950), 697.

"One of the most fateful attitudes of contemporary thought is the naive belief that all political and social problems could and should be solved immediately, i.e. the optimistic belief 'that there is a ready-made, immediate answer to all problems and misfortunes, and that only the malevolence of enemies stands in the way of its being instantly applied'. No virtue is so rare in our society as patience. For this reason our society has been called the *instant society*. But as Georg Christoph Lichtenberg rightly remarks: 'Wanting to do everything at once destroys everything at once.; The idea that the social problems of mankind and all other problems could be solved quickly and immediately, that the conflict-free society could be established if people only decided unreservedly to destroy completely all the present structures, is just as naive and unrealistic as the chiliastic expectation that with the second coming of Christ everything will be changed at once. Peace and justice will be the fruit of the spiritual rebirth of mankind, a complete change in the consciousness of the new man, a new order and a laborious process of construction."
 Udo Schaefer, *The Imperishable Dominion: The Bahá'í Faith and the Future of Mankind*, trans. Janet Rawling-Keitel, David Hopper, Patricia Crampton (Oxford: George Ronald, 1983), 141.

☐

Goals for Mankind: A Report to the Club of Rome on the New Horizons of Global Community by Ervin Laszlo et al., reviews the role of major religions in establishing peace and unity. In their review the authors "analyze only the religions which influence vast numbers of people" although they recognize, at the same time, "that several smaller religious groups exercise important and relevant forms of influence (the principle aim of the Bahá'í Faith, for example, is world unification)."

☐

"Judaism sees man as a partner with God in the ongoing work of creation. The exalted Jewish conception of man as 'the image of God' calls man to the creative human tasks which reflect the labors of the Divine Creator himself."
 Ervin Laszlo, et al., *Goals for Mankind: A Report of the Club of Rome on the New Horizons of Global Community* (New York: E.P. Dutton, 1977), 370.

☐

"... the Christian Churches are making remarkable progress in overcoming ancient feuds among themselves as well as with non-Christians and even atheists, and encouraging the growth of a new humanism which embraces all people."
 Laszlo, 376.

"Islam possesses rich moral and spiritual resources for the future of mankind. The emphasis of Islam on human fraternity, its articulation of the universal dimension of what it means to be human, its conviction that man is always *homo religiosus* and that, by God's grace, he can make the earth his provisional home—these are recurring themes in the history and thought of Islam, and they could inspire greater solidarity between Moslems and the rest of the world community."
Laszlo, 380.

☐

"Central to Hinduism is the cosmic principle that the unity of the Creator's marvelous phenomena is expressed through diversity, as the different instruments and harmonies blend in an orchestra. Any man can develop his *atman* (soul) and attain the cosmic consciousness by his own efforts. He does not need to believe in anything, even in God, in order to set out on this path. He simply has to tread the path, for when he gets to his destination, he will 'know'.

"Hinduism, like most of the great religions, affirms that man has free will. He can attune himself to the cosmic harmony, thus expressing creativity (goodness); he can remain inert; or he can behave in a destructive way, thus expressing evil."
Laszlo, 383.

☐

"Identification with others is cultivated by Buddhists in meditations specifically devoted to the heightening of capacity for loving-kindness and the corollary virtues, compassion, joy in the joy of others, and impartiality."
Laszlo, 388.

☐

"The Chinese tradition embodied in Confucianism and Taoism holds a unified concept of man in relation to other men in society, and to other things in nature. There is an interdependence among all things and all acts, both psychological and physical . . . ."
Laszlo, 391.

☐

"This African sense of community could be instrumental in extending the solidarity of Africans from the local village and tribe not only to their newly independent nations, but to the African continent and beyond that to mankind as a whole."
Laszlo, 393.

The Golden Rule

"The teaching that we should treat others as we ourselves would wish to be treated, an ethic variously repeated in all the great religions . . . ."

Buddhism:
"Hurt not others in ways that you yourself would find hurtful."
Udana-Varqa, 5:18.

□

Zoroastrianism:
"That nature only is good when it shall not do unto another whatever is not good for its own self."
Dadistan-i Dinik, 94:5.

□

Judaism:
"What is hateful to you, do not to your fellow men. That is the entire Law, all the rest is commentary."
The Talmud, Shabbat, 31a.

□

Hinduism:
"This is the sum of all true righteousness: deal with others as thou wouldst thyself be dealt by. Do nothing to thy neighbour which thou wouldst not have him do to thee after."
The Mahabharata.

□

Christianity:
"As ye would that men should do to you, do ye also to them likewise."
Luke 6:31.

"All things whatsoever ye would that men should do to you, do ye even so to them: For this is the law and the prophets."
Matthew 7:12.

Islam:
"No one of you is a believer until he desires for his brother that which he desires for himself."
Sunnah.

☐

Taoism:
The good man "ought to pity the malignant tendencies of others; to rejoice over their excellence; to help them in their straits; to regard their gains as if they were his own, and their losses in the same way."
The Thai-Shang, 3.

☐

Confucianism:
"Surely it is the maxim of loving-kindness: Do not unto others that you would not have them do unto you."
Analects, XV, 23.

☐

Bahá'í:
"It is Our wish and desire that every one of you may become a source of all goodness unto men, and an example of uprightness to mankind. Beware lest ye prefer yourselves above your neighbours."
Bahá'u'lláh, *Gleanings*, 315.

"Blessed is he who preferreth his brother before himself."
Bahá'u'lláh, *Tablets of Bahá'u'lláh*, 71.

"And among the teachings of Bahá'u'lláh is voluntary sharing of one's property with others among mankind. This voluntary sharing is greater than equality, and consists in this, that man should not prefer himself to others, but rather should sacrifice his life and property for others."
'Abdu'l-Bahá, *Selections from the Writings of 'Abdu'l-Bahá*, (Haifa: Bahá'í World Centre, 1978), 302.

Substitute Faiths

"How tragic is the record of the substitute faiths that the worldly-wise of our age have created. In the massive disillusionment of entire populations who have been taught to worship at their altars can be read history's irreversible verdict on their value."

". . . It would be perhaps impossible to find a nation of people not in a state of crisis today. The materialism, the lack of true religion and the consequent baser forces in human nature which are being released, have brought the whole world to the brink of probably the greatest crisis it has ever faced or will have to face."
    Written on behalf of Shoghi Effendi, *Bahá'í News* 304, 2.

□

"Humanity has, alas, with increasing insistence, preferred, instead of acknowledging and adoring the Spirit of God as embodied in His religion in this day, to worship those false idols, untruths and half-truths, which are obscuring its religions, corrupting its spiritual life, convulsing its political institutions, corroding its social fabric, and shattering its economic structure.

"Not only have the peoples of the earth ignored, and some of them even assailed, a Faith which is at once the essence, the promise, the reconciler, and the unifier of all religions, but they have drifted away from their own religions, and set up on their subverted altars other gods wholly alien not only to the spirit but to the traditional forms of their ancient faiths. . . .

"God Himself has indeed been dethroned from the hearts of men, and an idolatrous world passionately and clamorously hails and worships the false gods which its own idle fancies have fatuously created, and its misguided hands so impiously exalted. The chief idols in the desecrated temple of mankind are none other than the triple gods of Nationalism, Racialism, and Communism, at whose altars governments and peoples, whether democratic or totalitarian, at peace or at war, of the East or of the West, Christian or Islamic, are, in various forms and in different degrees, now worshipping. Their high priests are the politicians and the worldly-wise, the so-called sages of the age; their sacrifice, the flesh and blood of the slaughtered multitudes; their incantations, outworn shibboleths and insidious and irreverent formulas; their incense, the smoke of anguish that ascends from the lacerated hearts of the bereaved, the maimed, and the homeless.

"The theories and policies, so unsound, so pernicious, which deify the state and exalt the nation above mankind, which seek to subordinate the sister races of the world to one single race, which discriminate between the black and the white, and which tolerate the dominance of one privileged class over all others—these are the dark, the false, and crooked doctrines for which any man or people who believes in them, or acts upon them, must, sooner or later, incur the wrath and chastisement of God."

    Shoghi Effendi, *Guidance for Today and Tomorrow* (London: Bahá'í Publishing Trust, 1953), 158–160.

Disarmament

"Banning nuclear weapons, prohibiting the use of poison gases or outlawing germ warfare will not remove the root causes of war."

"O rulers of the Earth! Be reconciled among yourselves, that ye may need no more armaments save in a measure to safeguard your territories and dominions. Beware lest ye disregard the counsel of the All-Knowing, the Faithful.

"Be united, O kings of the earth, for thereby will the tempests of discord be stilled amongst you, and your people find rest, if ye be of them that comprehend. Should any one among you take up arms against another, rise ye all against him, for this is naught but manifest justice."
Bahá'u'lláh, *The Proclamation of Bahá'u'lláh* (Haifa: Bahá'í World Centre, 1972), 12–13.

□

"The Great Being, wishing to reveal the prerequisites of the peace and tranquillity of the world and the advancement of its peoples, hath written: The time must come when the imperative necessity for the holding of a vast, an all-embracing assemblage of men will be universally realized. The rulers and kings of the earth must needs attend it, and, participating in its deliberations, must consider such ways and means as will lay the foundations of the world's Great Peace amongst men. Such a peace demandeth that the Great Powers should resolve, for the sake of the tranquillity of the peoples of the earth, to be fully reconciled among themselves. Should any king take up arms against another, all should unitedly arise and prevent him. If this be done, the nations of the world will no longer require armaments, except for the purpose of preserving the security of their realms and of maintaining internal order within their territories. . . ."
Bahá'u'lláh, *Gleanings*, 249.

□

"Compose your differences, and reduce your armaments, that the burden of your expenditures may be lightened, and that your minds and hearts

may be tranquillized. Heal the dissensions that divide you, and ye will no longer be in need of any armaments except what the protection of your cities and territories demandeth."
    Bahá'u'lláh, *Gleanings*, 250–251.

☐

"It is their duty [the Sovereigns] to convene an all-inclusive assembly, which either they themselves or their ministers will attend, and to enforce whatever measures are required to establish unity and concord amongst men. They must put away the weapons of war, and turn to the instruments of universal reconstruction. Should one king rise up against another, all the other kings must arise to deter him. Arms and armaments will, then, be no more needed beyond that which is necessary to insure the internal security of their respective countries .

    "In this land [Persia], every time men are conscripted for the army, a great terror seizeth the people. Every nation augmenteth, every year, its forces, for their ministers of war are insatiable in their desire to add fresh recruits to their battalions."
    Bahá'u'lláh, *Epistle to the Son of the Wolf* (Wilmette, Ill.: Bahá'í Publishing Trust, 1971), 30–31.

☐

"It is vitally important, too, that the discussion of the peaceful use of nuclear technology be divorced from questions of nuclear armaments where there is no necessary connection between the two. To use, for example, illustrations of atomic destruction in literature which treats domestic industrial questions is morally indefensible; a responsible public needs accurate information to allay their unfounded fears as much as they need assurance that the possible misuses of the products of the nuclear fuel cycle or its strategic risks have not been dismissed."
    Bahá'í Community of Canada, Submission to the Interfaith Program for Public Awareness of Nuclear Issues, November 1, 1984.

Declarations and Conventions of the United Nations

"Despite the obvious short-comings of the United Nations, the more than two score declarations and conventions adopted by that organization, even where governments have not yet been enthusiastic in their commitment, have given ordinary people a sense of a new lease on life."

- Convention against discrimination in education (UNESCO)
- Convention concerning discrimination in respect of employment and occupation (ILO)
- Convention concerning freedom of the right to organize
- Convention for the protection of cultural property in the event of armed conflict
- Convention for the suppression of the traffic in persons and of the exploitation of the prostitution of others
- Convention on fishing and conservation of the living resources of the high seas
- Convention on consular relations
- Convention on diplomatic relations
- Convention on international liability for damage caused by space objects
- Convention on registration of objects launched into outer space
- Convention on special missions
- Convention on the abolition of slavery
- Convention on the continental shelf
- Convention on the elimination of all forms of racial discrimination
- Convention on the high seas
- Convention on the international rights of correction
- Convention on the law of treaties
- Convention on the prevention and punishment of crimes against international persons, including diplomatic agents
- Convention on the political rights of women
- Convention on the prevention and punishment of the crime of genocide
- Convention on the privileges and immunities of the U.N.

- Convention on the prohibition of the development, production and stockpiling of bacteriological (biological) and toxic weapons and on their destruction
- Convention on the recovery abroad of maintenance
- Convention on the representation of states in their relations with international organizations of a universal character
- Convention on the suppression and punishment of the crime of apartheid
- Convention on the territorial sea and the contiguous zone
- Convention relating to the status of refugees
- Universal copyright convention
- Universal declaration of human rights
- Declaration of legal principles governing the activities of states in the exploitation and use of outer space
- Declaration of principles governing the sea-bed and the ocean floor, and the subsoil thereof, beyond the limits of national jurisdiction
- Declaration of principles of international law concerning friendly relations and cooperation among states
- Declaration on the elimination of all forms of racial discrimination
- Declaration on the elimination of discrimination against women
- Declaration on the granting of independence to colonial countries and peoples
- Declaration on the inadmissibility of intervention on the domestic affairs of states and the protection of their independence and sovereignty
- Declaration on the prohibition of the use of nuclear and thermonuclear weapons
- Declaration on social progress and development
- Declaration on territorial asylum
- Declaration on the promoting among youth of the ideal of peace, mutual respect and understanding between peoples
- Declaration on the rights of the child
- Declaration on the strengthening of international security

☐

It is important to note that in passing a declaration or convention rather than a resolution, the members of the United Nations want to make the point that these specific issues are of particular concern. Nevertheless, like U.N. resolutions, U.N. conventions and declarations are merely recommandatory in nature with no instrumentalities of enforcement.

☐

Further information concerning the declarations and the conventions and their effectiveness can be had from the following sources:
    Bokor-Szego, H. *The Role of the United Nations in International Legislation*. Amsterdam: North-Holland, 1978.

Murphy, J.F. *The United Nations and the Control of International Violence*. Totowa, N.J.: Rowman & Allanheld, 1982.

Barriers to Peace:
Racism

"*Racism, one of the most baneful and persistent evils, is a major barrier to peace.*"

Article 1
"All human beings are born free and equal in dignity and rights. They are endowed with reason and conscience and should act toward one another in a spirit of brotherhood."

Article 2
"Everyone is entitled to all the rights and freedoms set forth in this Declaration, without distinction of any kind, such as race, colour, sex, language, religion, political or other opinion, national or social origin, property, birth or other status. . . ."
From the Universal Declaration of Human Rights. Adopted by the General Assembly of the U.N., 10 December, 1948.

☐

"So I say to you, my friends, that even though we must face the difficulties of today and tomorrow, I still have a dream. It is a dream deeply rooted in the American dream that one day this nation will rise up and live out the true meaning of its creed—we hold these truths to be self evident, that all men are created equal.

"I have a dream that one day on the red hills of Georgia, sons of former slaves and sons of former slave-owners will be able to sit down together at the table of brotherhood. . . .

"I have a dream my four little children will one day live in a nation where they will not be judged by the color of their skin but by the content of their character. I have a dream today!"
Martin Luther King, Jr., From a speech made in Washington, D.C., 28 August, 1963.

Barriers to Peace
Disparity Between Rich and Poor

"The inordinate disparity between rich and poor, a source of acute suffering, keeps the world in a state of instability, virtually on the brink of war."

"More than one-fifth of the people of the world are undernourished or hungry, at least 500–600 million, possibly 1 billion."
   P. Stephenson, *Handbook of World Development: The Guide to the Brandt Report* (Harlow: Longman, 1981), 31.

☐

"The World Bank estimates that 800 million people are living in destitution, so 'almost 40 per cent of the people in the South are surviving...with income judged insufficient to secure the basic necessities of life.'
   "...the world's military spending dwarfs any spending on development. Total military expenditures are approaching $450 billion a year, of which over half is spent by the Soviet Union and the United States, while annual spending on official development aid is only $20 billion."
   Brandt Commission, *North-South: A Programme for Survival* (London: Pan Books, 1980), 117.

☐

In 1985, total military spending was close to $800 billion U.S.
   [Editor's note]

☐

"...the United States, with only 6 percent of the world's population, consumes about 30 percent of the total energy production of the world and comparable amounts of other resources, and the rest of the 'haves', although only about half as prodigal as the United States, still consume resources far out of proportion to their population; conversely, per capita consumption of resources in the Third World ranges from one-tenth to one-hundredth that in the 'have' countries."
   W. Ophuls, *Ecology and the Politics of Scarcity* (San Francisco: W.H. Freeman, 1977), 210–211.

"We too often forget that even today the depth of human suffering is immense. Every two seconds of this year [1983] a child will die of hunger or disease. And no statistic can express what it is to see even one child die."
    Brandt Commission, *Common Crisis: North-South Cooperation for World Recovery* (London: Pan Books, 1983), 9–10.

Barriers to Peace
Unbridled Nationalism

"Unbridled nationalism, as distinguished from a sane and legitimate patriotism, must give way to a wider loyalty, to the love of humanity as a whole."

"Lo, soul! seest thou not god's purpose from
  the first?
The earth to be spann'd, connected by net-
  work,
The people to become brothers and sisters,
The races, neighbors, to marry and be given
  in marriage,
The oceans to be cross'd, the distant brought
  near,
The lands to be welded together."
  Walt Whitman (1819–1892), "Passage to India."

☐

"All states should put aside mutual suspicion and unite in one sole society or rather family of peoples, both to guarantee their own independence and safeguard order in the civil concert of peoples."
  Pope Benedict XV, *International Reconciliation*, 1920.

☐

"I now understand that my welfare is only possible if I acknowledge my unity with all the people of the world without exception."
  Leo Tolstoy, *What I Believe*, (1895).

☐

"Men exist for the sake of one another. Teach them then or bear with them."
  Marcus Aurelius (121–180) *Meditations*, 8:59.

"We were born to unite with our fellow men, and to join in community with the human race."
    Marcus Tullius Cicero (106-43-B.C.) *De finibus*, 4.

Barriers to Peace
Religious Strife

"Religious strife, throughout history, has been the cause of innumerable wars and conflicts, a major blight to progress, and is increasingly abhorrent to people of all faiths and no faith."

"The religion of God is for love and unity; make it not the cause of enmity and dissension."
Bahá'u'lláh, *Tablets of Bahá'u'lláh, 220.*

☐

"Religious conflict is not just a nuisance but is a sin. It is sinful because it arouses the wild beast in Human Nature. . . it is sinful because no one has a right to stand between another human soul and God."
A. J. Toynbee, *An Historian's Approach to Religion* (New York: Oxford University Press, 1956).

☐

"A time may come when the local heritages of the different historical nations, civilizations and religions will have coalesced into a common heritage of the whole human family. . . .The missions of the highest religions are not competitive; they are complementary."
Toynbee, *An Historian's Approach to Religion.*

Important Prerequisites for Peace
Equality of the Sexes

"*The emancipation of women, the achievement of full equality between the sexes, is one of the most important, though less acknowledged prerequisites of peace.*"

"And among the teachings of Bahá'u'lláh is the equality of women and men. The world of humanity has two wings—one is women and the other men. Not until both wings are equally developed can the bird fly. Should one wing remain weak, flight is impossible. Not until the world of women becomes equal to the world of men in the acquisition of virtues and perfections, can success and prosperity be attained as they ought to be."
'Abdu'l-Bahá. *Selections from the Writings of 'Abdu'l-Bahá*, 302.

☐

"Women have equal rights with men upon earth; in religion and society they are a very important element. As long as women are prevented from attaining their highest possibilities, so long will men be unable to achieve the greatness which might be theirs."
'Abdu'l-Bahá, *Paris Talks*, 133.

☐

"In the world of humanity we find a great difference; the female sex is treated as though inferior, and is not allowed equal rights and privileges. This condition is due not to nature, but to education. In the Divine Creation there is no such distinction. Neither sex is superior to the other in the sight of God. Why then should one sex assert the inferiority of the other, withholding just rights and privileges as though God had given His authority for such a course of action? If women received the same educational advantages as those of men, the result would demonstrate the equality of capacity of both for scholarship."
'Abdu'l-Bahá, *Paris Talks*, 161.

Important Prerequisites for Peace
Universal Education

"The cause of universal education . . . deserves the utmost support that the governments of the world can lend it."

"Bend your minds and wills to the education of the peoples and kindreds of the earth, that haply the dissensions that divide it may, through the power of the Most Great Name, be blotted out from its face, and all mankind be the upholders of one Order, and the inhabitants of one City."
    Bahá'u'lláh, *Gleanings*, 333–334.

☐

". . . man has a purpose, not just to be pure and finer than others, but to use his spiritual riches, his aesthetic greatness, in the service of others. Powers must be expressed, and so complete the cycle of relationship. This point of view must be taken into account not only in the practise of life, but in education. . . . Education should no longer be mostly imparting of knowledge, but must take a new path, seeking the release of human potentialities."
    Maria Montessori, *Education for a New World* (Madras: Kalakshetra Publications, 1963), 48.

☐

"One-third of the adults in the South were literate in 1950: now it is a little over half. . . .There are still 34 countries where illiteracy is over 80 per cent: and in the following 14 countries it is 90 per cent or more—Afghanistan, Chad, Guinea, Ethiopia, Gambia, Guinea-Bissau, Mali, Mauritania, Niger, Oman, Senegal, Sierra Leone, Togo and Upper Volta (Burkina Fasso)."
    P. Stephenson (1982), 40.

☐

	# *Illiterate*	% *of adults (over 15)*
1950	700 million	44%
1970	758 million	32.4%
1980	824 million	28.9%

UNESCO Courier (May 1983), 9.

"Since wars begin in the minds of men, it is in the minds of men that the defenses of peace must be constructed."
Constitution of UNESCO.

□

"Psychological causes of war are preventable. With a program of universal education based on the principles of the oneness of mankind, new generations can be raised to see the world as 'but one country and mankind its citizens.'"
H. Danesh, *Unity: The Creative Foundation for Peace.*

Important Prerequisites for Peace
Improved Global Communication

"A fundamental lack of communication between peoples seriously undermines efforts towards world peace. Adopting an international auxiliary language would go far to resolving this problem and necessitates the most urgent attention."

"A universal language would make intercourse possible with every nation. Thus it would be needful to know two languages only, the mother tongue and the universal speech. The latter would enable a man to communicate with any and every man in the world!

"A third language would not be needed. To be able to talk with a member of any race and country without requiring an interpreter, how helpful and restful to all!"
  'Abdu'l-Bahá, *Paris Talks*, 156.

☐

". . .the improvement of communications among the peoples of the world is essential. The structures of world peace are often built in the minds of ordinary people, based on feelings of security and confidence in a just and rational world. If people are insecure about their neighbours and do not know their nature or intentions, it is only too easy to generate fears, whether justified or unjustified."
  Javier Perez de Cuellar, Secretary-General of the United Nations
  UN Chronicle (Sept. 1982), 31.

Unity: The Cardinal Prerequisite for Peace

"World order can be founded only on an unshakeable consciousness of the oneness of mankind, a spiritual truth which all the human sciences confirm."

"The Bahá'í Faith recognizes the unity of God and of His Prophets, upholds the principle of an unfettered search after truth, condemns all forms of superstition and prejudice, teaches that the fundamental purpose of religion is to promote concord and harmony, that it must go hand-in-hand with science, and that it constitutes the sole and ultimate basis of a peaceful, an ordered and progressive society. It inculcates the principle of equal opportunity, rights and privileges for both sexes, advocates compulsory education, abolishes extremes of poverty and wealth, exalts work performed in the spirit of service to the rank of worship, recommends the adoption of an auxiliary international language, and provides the necessary agencies for the establishment and safeguarding of a permanent and universal peace."
　　Shoghi Effendi, *Selected Writings of Shoghi Effendi*, 1–2.

□

"Before peace comes without, in the great arena of men's joint life on this planet, a measure of it must first come within. How can we enforce new laws, support far-reaching international policies, drive forward unitedly towards our goal of world cooperation and co-ordination, freedom from fear, unless we ourselves each set our own compass on something firm to steer by and seek to know what is a human being's real place in the scheme of things? What are his potentialities, what is required of him? And let each one ask himself, what can I do myself?"
　　Rúhíyyih Rabbani, *Prescription for Living* (London: George Ronald, 1950), 203–204.

□

"Over a century ago, Bahá'u'lláh stated that 'the well-being of mankind, its peace and security are unattainable unless and until its unity is firmly established.' The call of Bahá'u'lláh for the unity of mankind also has its counterpart at the individual level. On a personal level, we are likewise challenged with the task of attaining a state of unity, not only the inner unity necessary for creating a full and integrated life for ourselves, but also an interpersonal unity, a unity between ourselves and the members of our family, society, country, and the world. This is a call for a condition of unity which will ultimately encompass the whole earth.

"To achieve this high level of individual and collective unity, we require a new mind-set, new approaches to the use of power and love in our relationships, a new perspective on freedom, justice, and equality, a new understanding of the roles of religion and science in human affairs, and a new approach to the issues of the equality of men and women, among others . The accomplishment of world peace, as Bahá'u'lláh attests, is possible only if we are willing to humble ourselves and approach this task with a spirit of humanity and receptivity:

> O contending peoples and kindreds of the earth! Set your faces towards unity, and let the radiance of its lights shine upon you. Gather ye together, and for the sake of God resolve to root out whatever is the source of contention amongst you. Then will the effulgence of the world's great Luminary envelop the whole earth, and its habitants become the citizens of one city, the occupants of one and the same throne."

H. Danesh, *Unity: The Creative Foundation for Peace*, Citation of Bahá'u'lláh from *Gleanings*, 217.

☐

"The things which make men alike are finer and better than the things that keep them apart, and these basic likenesses, if they are properly accentuated, easily transcend the less essential difference of race, language, creed and tradition. . . .

"You ask what I consider to be the greatest need of the world today. . . I would put it in one word, *understanding*—understanding between individuals, classes, races, nations. Literature, history and mechanics are bringing it about much more rapidly today. Are not nations simply families living together, learning to adjust themselves to each other for the best good for the greatest number? . . .

"The problems of the world which are caused by wrong mental attitudes are returning to the heart and mind of man and the solution must come through changed mental attitudes."

Jane Addams, quoted in " 'Abdu'l-Bahá's Historic Meeting with Jane Addams" by Ruth J. Moffat, *The Bahá'í World* 6 (1934–1936), 681–682.

Towards a
New World Order

"The League of Nations, the United Nations, and the many organizations and agreements produced by them have unquestionably been helpful in attenuating some of the negative effects of international conflicts, but they have shown themselves incapable of preventing war."

"Far from aiming at the subversion of the existing foundations of society, it [the world-wide law of Bahá'u'lláh] seeks to broaden its basis, to remold its institutions in a manner consonant with the needs of an ever-changing world. It can conflict with no legitimate allegiances, nor can it undermine essential loyalties. Its purpose is neither to stifle the flame of a sane and intelligent patriotism in men's hearts, nor to abolish the system of national autonomy so essential if the evils of excessive centralization are to be avoided. It does not ignore, nor does it attempt to suppress, the diversity of ethnical origins, of climate, of history, of language and tradition, of thought and habit, that differentiate the peoples and nations of the world. It calls for a wider loyalty, for a larger aspiration than any that has animated the human race. It insists upon the subordination of national impulses and interests to the imperative claims of a unified world. It repudiates excessive centralization on one hand and disclaims all attempts at uniformity on the other. Its watchword is unity in diversity."
Shoghi Effendi, *The World Order of Bahá'u'lláh*, 41–42.

□

"The unity of the human race, as envisaged by Bahá'u'lláh, implies the establishment of a world commonwealth in which all nations, races, creeds and classes are closely and permanently united, and in which the autonomy of its state members and the personal freedom and initiative of the individuals that compose them are definitely and completely safeguarded. This commonwealth must, as far as we can visualize it, consist of a world legislature, whose members will, as the trustees of the whole of mankind, ultimately control the entire resources of all the component nations, and will enact such laws as shall be required to regulate the life, satisfy the needs and adjust the relationships of all races and

peoples. A world executive, backed by an international Force, will carry out the decisions arrived at, and apply the laws enacted by, this world legislature, and will safeguard the organic unity of the whole commonwealth. A world tribunal will adjudicate and deliver its compulsory and final verdict in all and any disputes that may arise between the various elements constituting this universal system."
  Shoghi Effendi, *The World Order of Bahá'u'lláh*, 203.

□

"A world federal system, ruling the whole earth and exercising unchallengeable authority over its unimaginably vast resources, blending and embodying the ideals of both the East and the West, liberated from the curse of war and its miseries, and bent on the exploitation of all the available sources of energy on the surface of the planet, a system in which Force is made the servant of Justice, whose life is sustained by its universal recognition of God...."
  Shoghi Effendi, *The World Order of Bahá'u'lláh*, 204.

□

"A mechanism of world inter-communication will be devised, embracing the whole planet, freed from national hindrances and restrictions, and functioning with marvellous swiftness and perfect regularity. A world metropolis will act as the nerve center of a world civilization, the focus towards which the unifying forces of life will converge and from which its energizing influences will radiate. A world language will either be invented or chosen from among the existing languages and will be taught in the schools of all the federated nations as an auxiliary to their mother tongue. A world script, a world literature, a uniform and universal system of currency, of weights and measures, will simplify and facilitate intercourse and understanding among the nations and races of mankind. In such a world society, science and religion, the two most potent forces in human life, will be reconciled, will cooperate, and will harmoniously develop. The press will, under such a system, while giving full scope to the expression of the diversified views and convictions of mankind, cease to be mischievously manipulated by vested interests, whether private or public, and will be liberated from the influence of contending governments and peoples. The economic resources of the world will be organized, its sources of raw materials will be tapped and fully utilized, its markets will be coordinated and developed, and the distribution of its products will be equitably regulated.

  "National rivalries, hatreds, and intrigues will cease, and racial animosity and prejudice will be replaced by racial amity, understanding and cooperation. The causes of religious strife will be permanently removed, economic barriers and restrictions will be completely abolished, and the inordinate distinction between classes will be obliterated. Destitution on the one hand, and gross accumulation of ownership on the other, will disappear. The enormous energy dissipated and wasted on war, whether economic or political, will be consecrated to such ends as will extend the range of human inventions and technical development, to the increase of the productivity of mankind, to the extermination of disease, to the extension of scientific research, to the raising of the standard of physical health, to the sharpening and refinement of the human brain, to the exploitation of the unused and unsuspected resources of the planet, to the prolongation of human life, and to the furtherance of any other agency that can stimulate the intellectual, the moral, and spiritual life of the entire human race."

Shoghi Effendi, *The World Order of Bahá'u'lláh*, 203–204.

Consultation and Conflict Resolution

" 'Consultation bestows greater awareness and transmits conjecture into certitude. It is a shining light which, in a dark world, leads the way and guides.' "

"Underlying all the laws and community structures in the Bahá'í Faith is a group decision-making process called 'consultation.' Essentially, Bahá'í consultation involves a frank but loving exchange of opinions by members of a group with a view towards the determination of the truth of some matter and the establishment of a genuine group consensus. It is no exaggeration to say that virtually every member of the Bahá'í Faith is a student of the process of consultation....

"One of the best-known summaries of the Bahá'í pattern of consultation is to be found in a passage from 'Abdu'l-Bahá's writings which has become a working document for Bahá'í national and local spiritual assemblies:

> The first condition is absolute love and harmony amongst the members of the assembly. They must be wholly free from estrangement and must manifest in themselves the Unity of God, for they are the waves of one sea, the drops of one river, the stars of one heaven. They must when coming together turn their faces to the Kingdom on High and ask aid from the Realm of glory. They must then proceed with the utmost devotion, courtesy, dignity, care and moderation to express their views. They must in every matter search out the truth and not insist upon their own opinion. For stubbornness and persistence in one's views will lead ultimately to discord and wrangling and the truth will remain hidden. The honored members must with all freedom express their own thoughts, and it is in no wise permitted for one to belittle the thought of another, nay, he must with moderation set forth the truth, and should differences of opinion arise a majority of voices must prevail, and all must obey and submit to the majority. It is again not permitted that any one of the honored members object to or censure, whether in or out of the meeting, any decision arrived at previously, though that decision be

not right, for such criticism would prevent any decision from being enforced.... Should they... endeavor to fulfill these conditions the Grace of the Holy Spirit shall be vouchsafed unto them, and that assembly shall become the center of the Divine blessings, the hosts of Divine confirmation shall come to their aid, and they shall day by day receive a new effusion of Spirit."

Hatcher/Martin, 161-163. Citation of 'Abdu'l-Bahá quoted by Shoghi Effendi in *Bahá'í Administration* (Wilmette, Illinois: Bahá'í Publishing Trust, 1974), 22-23.

☐

"The basis which Bahá'u'lláh creates for the training and development of the individual is consultation. It applies to all areas of human association, including the family. Bahá'ís are encouraged to speak with 'absolute freedom' while seeing that 'no occasion for ill-feeling or discord may arise.' They are urged to see their ideas as contributions to the group and to struggle to detach themselves from personal interest in them once they have been presented. Criticism of others as a means of social control is strongly discouraged, whether it occurs in consultative situations or individual encounters. The spirit of trust that communication of this kind produces, in turn engenders real love and a profound sense of unity."

H. Danesh, "Universal Man and Prejudiced Man," *World Order* (Spring, 1974), 23-24.

☐

"The Bahá'í community is made up of people drawn from a bewildering variety of racial, cultural and religious backgrounds, living in over 100,000 communities of various size spread across the face of the earth. Some of the issues facing it are vexing and painful in the extreme. Despite the widely different circumstances to which Bahá'í activity must adapt, our community has found it entirely possible to function as a united body on those aspects of life which we regard as essential to the well-being of our members. The key to the achievement of this unity has been a body of consultative principles derived from the Scriptures of our Faith which forms the basis of our administrative and individual lives. We hope it is not inappropriate to share them with these hearings:

1. Freedom and opportunity for all those affected by a decision to participate in the consultative process.
2. A clear distinction between this broad consultation and the deliberations of the democratically elected body which must take responsibility for the decision.
3. Encouragement for every individual engaged in consultation to freely set forth his or her conscience.
4. The prohibition of any form of factionalism.
5. The responsibility of all those participating to exercise courtesy and moderation.

6. The moral obligation of all individuals in the consultative process to detach themselves from their own contribution, which, once it has been made, becomes a common possession.
7. Once a decision is taken, the community understands its role to be that of the constituency which wholeheartedly implements that decision.
8. Having had a vital role in the consultation, decision-making and implementation, individuals as well as decision-making bodies are obliged to constantly evaluate their work and, where necessary, revise their decision.

"Consensus can be achieved only when there is frank, open and sincere consultation by all parties involved, with a view towards discovering the real truth of the matter at hand, which can only emerge from the 'clash of differing opinions'. It is not only the process of consultation itself which is so important, but the spirit of seeking truth rather than merely juxtaposing irreconcilable and irreducible adversary opinions.

"When consultation is animated by the spirit of such sincere truth-seeking and safeguarded by a mutually-respected framework, the parties involved gradually lose their feelings of mutual mistrust. They no longer find it necessary or useful to assume exaggerated or one-sided 'bargaining positions' as hedges against future concessions. Nor do they fear becoming naive dupes manipulated by one side or the other. Having had an opportunity to express fully their concerns, and with the assurance that they are being listened to, they are much more inclined to accept the final consensus as fair and just. Lacking such an opportunity, they may reject the final decision even if equitable."

The Bahá'í Community of Canada, Submission to the Interfaith Program for Public Awareness of Nuclear Issues, November 1, 1984.

The Experience of the Bahá'í Community

"Together with the opposing tendency to warfare and self-aggrandizement against which it ceaselessly struggles, the drive towards unity is one of the dominant, pervasive features of life on the planet during the closing years of the twentieth century.

"The experience of the Bahá'í community may be seen as an example of this enlarging unity."

"The process of community-building is well advanced in the Bahá'í Faith. During the first century of its existence, the Bahá'í community was primarily concentrated in Persia where, as a proscribed and much persecuted minority, it had little opportunity to experiment with the teachings of its founder. Once the teaching plans were implemented under the direction of Shoghi Effendi, however, and particularly as these plans became global in scope, the collective life of the believers began to manifest some of these 'society-building' potentialities. Whether the Bahá'í Faith will ultimately become the inspiration and guiding force of a new advance in a world civilization, as have other revealed religions, is something only time will demonstrate. The important fact to note is that, as a result of the activities of the faith over the past 140 years, a global Bahá'í community has come into existence and is now rapidly expanding. An understanding of the Bahá'í Faith must include an appreciation of this important development."

Hatcher/Martin, 166–167.

☐

" 'All men,' said Bahá'u'lláh, 'are created to carry forward an ever-advancing civilization'. This is the standard and this is the goal. Conviction of one's worth in these terms brings a sense of responsibility to develop, to train, and to perfect one's talents; it leaves no place for the sluggard or the parasite. Yet the impulse to develop must never be expressed at the expense or by the exploitation of others. The working of this principle of individual worth and responsibility makes possible an important step in social maturity. It removes at least two of the great impediments to cooperation between human beings who must work together; the insecurity of the individuals to accept without hostility the differences in human capacity and ability."

    Elsie Austin, "Unity as a Way of Life," *The Bahá'í World* 11 (1946–1950), 696.

☐

"In 1936, outside the land of its birth, the Bahá'í Cause had only a few thousand followers, living in fewer than perhaps a thousand localities in approximately forty countries and territories of the globe. Its administrative structure consisted of ten National Spiritual Assemblies, several of them serving two or more countries at the same time, and fewer than 120 Local Spiritual Assemblies. Only a handful of these bodies were incorporated. At its World Centre in the Holy Land, near the burial places of the Báb and Bahá'u'lláh, external circumstances had made it impossible for the Cause to pursue more than a token development. To the great mass of the people of the world even the name of the movement was as yet unknown.

"Today, forty years later, the Bahá'í Cause is established in over 330 countries, territories, and major islands of the globe, from isolated villages in Canada's farthest Arctic to the remotest islands of the South Pacific. It includes in its embrace representatives of virtually every religious, racial, ethnic, national, and social group on earth. There are today as many National Bahá'í Assemblies as there were Local Assemblies in 1935, and the number of Local Assemblies now approaches twenty thousand, quite apart from the more than sixty thousand centers where Assemblies are being built by Bahá'í groups or by individual believers. Wherever this institutional development has occurred, the creation of Houses of Worship, schools, hospices and administrative headquarters, and the acquisition of other properties for such purposes, have followed. In 1963, on the one hundredth anniversary of Bahá'u'lláh's declaration of His mission, the members of the fifty-six National and Regional Spiritual Assemblies, of whom more than 280 gathered on the slopes of Mount Carmel, brought into existence, in what may well have been the first democratic global election in history, the crowning unity of the Administrative Order conceived by Bahá'u'lláh. That body took the name which Bahá'u'lláh had given it a century earlier, 'The Universal House of Justice.' Through the acquisition of consultative status in the non-governmental organizations of the United Nations, as well as through the continuously expanding recognition of its institutions and practices by scores of national and provincial Governments around the world, the Cause has secured those relationships with civil authority which are necessary to its various humanitarian purposes. Its literature, which in 1936 was translated into fewer than forty languages, can today be read in nearly 600, and includes not only the collected Writings of the

Founders and the commentaries of Shoghi Effendi as Guardian but also a vast range of works which elaborate the principles and teachings of the Cause for both the scholarly and the popular reader. Most recently an intensive program for the use of various communication media has begun in order to assure that the message of Bahá'u'lláh is as accessible to the illiterate seeker as it is to his more fortunate brother, as comprehensible to modern youth as it is to adults. The total phenomenon may well represent the most rapid expansion of a serious religious movement in modern history. . . .

"What are some of the features of this model which recommend it to . . . serious study. . . ? The first, and the one most relevant to our concerns here, is the model's *universality*. That is to say, that in attracting adherents from every race, class, and creed the process of assimilation has not occurred at the expense of cultural and spiritual diversity of its members. . . .

"It is a fact, established now through a century of experience, that a worldwide community can revere the Founders of all the great revealed religions equally; can draw for their devotions on the Bhagavad Gita, the Old Testament, The New Testament, and the Qur'án; can experience the precious benefits of 'interfaith dialogue' in the homeliest occasions of local community life and in the truest sense of that much abused phrase.

"A second feature of the model which has emerged from Bahá'u'lláh's Revelation is its success in remolding human conscience—in establishing a set of *universal moral standards* relevant to the age of mankind's maturity. Solely out of devotion to the founder of the Bahá'í Cause ordinary people in every part of the world have surrendered themselves to a process of education in ideals as comprehensive and challenging as the goals of the most advanced social reformers: the eradication of prejudices, the independent investigation of truth, the assurance of equality of opportunity to men and women, a program of universal education, the attainment of social justice, and the establishment of an effective world order, to name only a few of these ideals. The point is that these principles are not merely matters of sociological theory within the Bahá'í community but integral parts of the psychological pattern and emotional life in which generations of human beings, one generation after another, are being patiently and deliberately raised.

"Third, . . . Bahá'u'lláh's community enjoys its own *history*. It has its 'noble army of martyrs,' some twenty thousand of them, whose self-sacrifice won the unstinted admiration of Sir Francis Younghusband, when he first encountered their stories several decades ago. Apart from its lively interest in the spiritual giants of earlier Revelations it has its own archetypal heroes and saints (for whom its children are named), whose lives provide moral example, and whose spiritual achievements have already begun to evoke the first halting response of Bahá'í artists, writers, and musicians. Today, all around the world, an entire generation of Japanese, Italian, Bolivian, Ugandan, Canadian, and Persian children are being educated in this common tradition.

"Finally, there is the feature of the Bahá'í community which is related to the pivotal teaching of Bahá'u'lláh's Revelation: "The earth is but one country, and mankind its citizens." Bahá'u'lláh asserts that: "The well-being of mankind, its peace and security are unattainable unless and until its unity is firmly established." A feature of Bahá'u'lláh's model, therefore, which has enormous significance for the future, is the fact that it has passed safely through the first critical century of its history with its *unity* firmly intact. No single effort to create sects and factions has survived the generation which saw it appear. There is not, so far as I am aware, any other great movement in recorded history—religious, political, or social—of which this can be said. Time and again in all other forms of human association, the process of schism has taken hold in the early, vulnerable stages; and the originating impulse has had to continue its work through the activities of often contending parties and sects."

Douglas Martin, "Bahá'u'lláh's Model for World Unity," *The Bahá'í World* 16 (1973-1976), 682-684.

☐

"Within the framework of unity in diversity, the Bahá'í community creates a milieu conducive to the growth and maturation of both its individual members and its institutions. The Universal House of Justice, supreme governing body of the Bahá'í Faith, has compared the Bahá'í community to the human body:

In the human body, every cell, every organ, every nerve has its part to play. When all do so the body is healthy, vigorous, radiant and ready for every call made upon it. No cell, however humble, lives apart from the body, whether in serving it or receiving from it. This is true of the body of mankind in which God has endowed each humble being with ability and talent, and is supremely true of the body of the Bahá'í world community, for this body is already an organism, united in its aspirations, unified in its methods, seeking assistance and confirmation from the same source, and illumined with the conscious knowledge of its unity.

"In such a community there is a direct relationship between the individual's growth and the level of maturity of the ideas and the institutions with which he comes in contact. Among these are the institutions of the family and the Spiritual Assembly.

"The family, according to the teachings of Bahá'u'lláh, is the basic foundation of human society. It is within the secure setting of the family that the human infant receives care, love and nourishment, and is taught about himself, his fellow man and the world in general. Therefore the effect of the family on the development of the individual and his character is of immeasurable importance. . . .

"Within the framework of the Bahá'í community, . . . both the individual and the family are given the opportunity to free themselves from isolation and alienation, and at the same time to safeguard their individuality and privacy. This is accomplished by active and universal participation in the life of the community. The Bahá'í community, like all living organisms, has its own rhythm, self–regulating agencies and growth-inducing faculties. The rhythm of Bahá'í community life is established by its unique calendar. The year begins on the first day of spring and is divided into 19 months of 19 days each. On the first day of each month, Bahá'ís the world over take part in a Bahá'í Feast.

"The Feast fulfills an important part of the spiritual, intellectual, social and interpersonal needs of the individual. It provides a setting for meaningful and intimate collaboration between the individual, the community and Bahá'í institutions and it broadens the individual's world beyond the boundaries of his family, neighbourhood and work. . . .

"The rhythm and growth of Bahá'í community life is maintained and regulated by the institution of the Spiritual Assembly, which directs it in such a way that unity, cooperation, and a sense of fulfillment and joy are the outcome for all who take part."

    H. Danesh, "The Violence-Free Society," 18–20. Citation of the Universal House of Justice from *Wellspring of Guidance* (Wilmette: Bahá'í Publishing Trust, 1976), 37–38.

APPRECIATIONS

"Deeply impressed by the message contained in *The Promise of World Peace*, I would like—as a student of peace for many years—to explore three points that seem to me to be of particular significance. In a sense they all relate to our capacity for visioning, for creating images of a peaceful world. This is also a key characteristic of the Bahá'í Faith: you have to have an image of the desirable state of affairs, so clear, so commanding that the image itself becomes a live force. A part of our predicament is that only in short periods during and right after wars are the images of peace sufficiently commanding. In more peaceful periods it is as if we are yearning for war, producing images filled with strife and competition and selfishness, even elevating such characteristics to the status of 'law of human nature.'

"More precisely, I am thinking of three characteristic themes from what often refers to itself as the 'realism' school in social science in general, and policy sciences in particular: *peace through capacity to retaliate; development through trade according to comparative advantages; and evolution through self-interest and struggle for survival.* Needless to say, such themes will tend to be the credo of men more than women, of the middle-aged more than the old, of the powerful and privileged more than the powerless and discriminated, of the occident more than the orient. But the themes are very pervasive in this age which has taken on materialist individualism as its major faith. . . .

"The crowning achievement of this kind of thinking is the doctrine of national self-interest. That there is a selfish, competitive strain in individuals and nations alike, and that this may express itself in the direct violence released through offensive weaponry and the structural violence built into lopsided trade relations within and between countries—all this we know. Under certain conditions that is what comes out. But under other conditions the opposite comes out, altruism rather than egotism, cooperation rather than conflict and competition. Our task is to understand those conditions, not to proclaim that human behavior under adverse conditions is normal, and elevate that finding to a law of nature. In a jungle, it is probable that humans behave as one is supposed to behave in a jungle—although even the most elementary knowledge of biology in general and zoology in particular will inform us that in the struggle for survival there is cooperation as well as conflict, and that the Darwinist formula should make us look for the cooperative elements at least as much as the competitive and conflict-loaded themes.

"Let me finish on that note, simply by saying that some of the struggle for peace as envisaged in the Letter will have to take place in the corridors of social science. Inspired by a quest for a shared spirituality we have to struggle for better social sciences in general, and policy and peace sciences in particular."

Johan Galtung

□

"Both the thought that 'all nations and tribes shall become one nation' and the heartfelt sensation arising from the belief that 'religious and sectarian antagonism, hostility among races and peoples, and the differences among nations shall be banished' gladden the spirit and strengthen the belief in the achievement of peace.

"Ever since science and technology laid at our disposal the possibility to see our planet 'from afar' on a television screen, the feeling that the Earth is our common home began to emerge. Such a perception, which was then only visual, has since, through age and meditation, been transformed into a profound conviction and seen as a forthcoming reality. The truth of this reflection can be seen through concepts such as those expressed by Shoghi Effendi—most particularly when he asserts that the human species is faring through a transitional age, characteristic of the impetuosity and irrational instincts of youth: their folly, their extravagance, their pride, their self-confidence, their rebelliousness, and their aversion to discipline. He further states that the ages of childhood and infancy have passed not to return, 'whereas the Great Age is coming, as the consummation of all ages, the announcement of the entire human race's arrival at the stage of maturity.'

"The Bahá'í view provides a healthy perspective on all the senseless and unreasonable acts carried out by humanity throughout history, and upholds the promise of 'the Age of Ages' when humanity's painful experience will 'evolve into the wisdom and calmness of an imperturbable, universal and lasting peace; during which disagreement and segregation among the offspring of human beings will have given way to global reconciliation and total unification of the different elements which constitute human society.'

"To unite the world does not mean to undermine the loyalty due one's home country, but rather, I believe, to understand that interdependence among nations and the fact that the world has become a smaller place open up new possibilities for loyalty—to humanity as a whole. A world commonwealth is undoubtedly a response against egotism, against the desire for domination, against segregation among men, all of which subject people to bloodshed and sink the immense majority deep into hunger, dejection, and ignorance. The acceptance of humanity as an integrated unit '. . . shall introduce the spiritualization of the masses. . .' together with '. . . the final fusion of all races, creeds, classes, and nations, which shall proclaim the advent of its New World Order.' "

Rodrigo Carazo

About the Contributors

Rodrigo Carazo, distinguished statesman, educator, and politician, served as President of Costa Rica from 1978–1982. An advocate of global peace, he was the original proponent to the United Nations of a University for Peace, which was established in 1980. He now serves as the President of that institution.

Hossain Danesh currently serves as Chairman of the Executive Committee of the Association for Bahá'í Studies and Chairman of the Administrative Committee of the Bahá'í International Health Agency. A psychiatrist by profession, he was, until his recent election as General Secretary of the Bahá'í Community of Canada, associate professor of psychiatry and social medicine at the University of Ottawa.

Johan Galtung is currently a professor of world politics of peace and war at Princeton University. His distinguished academic career has seen him teach at over fifty institutions of higher learning in various parts of the world, and he has authored a large number of books and articles in his field.

Ervin Laszlo, member of the Club of Rome, has served as director for the United Nations Institute for Training and Research (UNITAR) and has most recently acted as an editor in chief of the *World Encyclopedia of Peace* published by Pergamon Press. He is an accomplished classical musician, editor of numerous scholarly journals, member of the advisory council of world-minded organizations such as Planetary Citizens, and has authored over thirty books throughout his distinguished and varied career.

Acknowledgements

The Association for Bahá'í Studies would like to acknowledge the contributions of the following individuals in the preparation of this book: Rocco Rossi, for his research of source materials; Ann Boyles, for editorial assistance; Louise Hanks and Lynn Weir for manuscript preparation; Stan Phillips for design, and layout; Russell Kerr for typesetting. For their review of the manuscript, the Association thanks Nancy Ackerman, Jane Graves, Peter Morgan, and Christine Zerbinis.

Select Bahá'í Bibliography

'Abdu'l-Bahá. *Paris Talks*, Addresses Given By 'Abdu'l-Bahá in Paris in 1911–1912. London: Bahá'í Publishing Trust, 1912. 11th ed. 1969.

———. *The Promulgation of Universal Peace*, Talks Delivered By 'Abdu'l-Bahá During His Visit to the United States and Canada in 1912. Compiled by Howard MacNutt. Wilmette: Bahá'í Publishing Trust, 1922–1925. 2d ed. 1982.

———. *The Secret of Divine Civilization*. Translated by Marzieh Gail and Ali-Kuli Khan. Wilmette: Bahá'í Publishing Trust, 1957. 3d ed. 1975.

Bahá'u'lláh and 'Abdu'l-Bahá. *Bahá'í World Faith: Selected Writings of Bahá'u'lláh and 'Abdu'l-Bahá*. Wilmette: Bahá'í Publishing Trust, 1943. Rev. ed. 1956.

Bahá'u'lláh. *Tablets of Bahá'u'lláh Revealed after the Kitáb-i-Aqdas.* Haifa: Bahá'í World Centre, 1978.

———. *The Kitáb-i-Iqán, The Book of Certitude*, Revealed by Bahá'u'lláh. Translated by Shoghi Effendi. Wilmette: Bahá'í Publishing Trust, 1931. 2d ed. 1950.

———. *The Proclamation of Bahá'u'lláh*. Haifa: Bahá'í World Centre, 1967.

Shoghi Effendi. *God Passes By*. Wilmette: Bahá'í Publishing Trust, 1944. 3d ed. 1974.

———. *The Promised Day Is Come*. Wilmette: Bahá'í Publishing Trust, 1941. 3d ed. 1980.

———. *The World Order of Bahá'u'lláh,* Selected Letters. Wilmette: Bahá'í Publishing Trust, 1938. 2d rev. ed. 1974.

Universal House of Justice. *Messages from the Universal House of Justice 1968–1973*. Wilmette: Bahá'í Publishing Trust, 1976.

———. *Wellspring of Guidance,* Messages 1963–1968. Wilmette: Bahá'í Publishing Trust, 1969. 2d ed. 1976.